YOUR FAITH,
YOUR LIFE

YOUR FAITH, YOUR LIFE

AN INVITATION TO THE EPISCOPAL CHURCH

JENIFER GAMBER

WITH BILL LEWELLIS

Morehouse Publishing
NEW YORK · HARRISBURG · DENVER

Unless otherwise noted, the Scripture quotations contained herein are from the New Revised Standard Version Bible, copyright © 1989 by the Division of Christian Education of the National Council of Churches of Christ in the U.S.A. Used by permission. All rights reserved.

Morehouse Publishing, 4775 Linglestown Road, Harrisburg, PA 17112

Morehouse Publishing, 445 Fifth Avenue, New York, NY 10016

Morehouse Publishing is an imprint of Church Publishing Incorporated.

Cover photograph: Christ Episcopal Church, Little Rock, Arkansas
(www.christchurchlr.org) by Jenna Dixon

Cover design by Laurie Klein Westhafer

Library of Congress Cataloging-in-Publication Data

Gamber, Jenifer.
    Your faith, your life : an invitation to the Episcopal Church / Jenifer Gamber
with Bill Lewellis.
        p. cm.
    Includes bibliographical references and index.
    ISBN 978-0-8192-2321-0 (pbk.)
    1. Episcopal Church.   I. Lewellis, Bill.   II. Title.
BX5930.3.G37 2009
283'.73—dc22

2008055219

Church Publishing Incorporated
445 Fifth Avenue
New York, NY 10016
www.churchpublishing.org

12 13 14   10 9 8 7 6 5 4 3

CONTENTS

Introduction:	Telling Secrets	1
Chapter One:	Transforming Questions	5

BE

Chapter Two:	Beginnings	13

SEEKING THE TRUE

— Be Attentive —

Chapter Three:	Bible Stories	28
Chapter Four:	History	51

— Be Intelligent —

Chapter Five:	Faith: Whom Do We Trust?	70

— Be Reasonable —

Chapter Six:	Navigating the Church	85

SEEKING THE GOOD

— Be Responsible —

Chapter Seven:	What Is God Calling You to Do?	105

SEEKING GOD

— Be in Love —

Chapter Eight:	Spirituality: Created for Prayer	125
Chapter Nine:	Worship: Responding to God's Blessings	148
Chapter Ten:	Sacraments	168
	Glossary	189
	References	200
	Acknowledgments	202

Introduction

Telling Secrets

Nearly twenty-five years ago, a committee planning a conference on "Spirituality and Mission" scheduled twelve workshops on spirituality for the morning, and twelve on mission for the afternoon. Separating the workshops in this way was a logistical — not a theological — decision. Still, we needed a way to preempt the message that spirituality and mission were separate but equal, and need not converge.

We discovered a story. A child wandered into a sculptor's studio and watched a master sculptor work with hammer and chisel on a large piece of marble. Marble chips flew in all directions. Months later the child returned. The block of marble had become a majestic and powerful Aslan-like lion. "How did you know," he asked the sculptor, "there was a lion in the marble?" "I knew," the sculptor replied, "because before I saw the lion in the marble, I saw him in my heart. The real secret, though, is that it was the lion in my heart who recognized the lion in the marble."

In *Clowning in Rome* Henri Nouwen told this story of the Christ within, who recognizes himself unformed in the disguises of the world, to illustrate the relationship between contemplation and action. We used it to show how clearly related spirituality and mission are.

The story also suggests to me as one who has worked in church communication for some forty years, that, for each of us as Christian disciples, our basic ministry is about God's word becoming flesh. Incarnation continues.

When I was a Roman Catholic priest working in the bishop's office of the Diocese of Allentown, I assisted that diocese's founding bishop at an ordination service where the preacher was the rector of the seminary.

Vincentian Father Bob Maloney — an insightful theologian and a friend — had a unique preaching style. He punctuated with whispers. You knew he was about to say something you needed to hear when he leaned forward and lowered his voice. It was effective. He leaned forward to whisper; the congregation leaned forward to hear. Bishop McShea didn't care for Bob's preaching style. As presider, he was seated behind the preacher, unable to hear the whispers. After the service, the bishop quipped to me, "Bob Maloney preaches like he's telling secrets."

I heard the quip as a mission statement: *tell secrets, tell what you have seen and heard*. Whenever we talk about God, or listen for God (whenever we worship or pray), we're in the realm of mystery...secret...the realm of the hidden yet revealed...a presence to be encountered somehow in our relationships and in the signs and symbols of our worship.

Christian thinkers have used both a Greek and a Latin word to talk about the hidden presence of the real — the partially veiled and partially unveiled presence of God — to refer to visible signs (persons, loved ones, the church, bread and wine) that communicate something of God's hidden presence.

From the Greek word *musterion* we get our English word "mystery" (secret, something hidden). It was translated into Latin as *sacramentum* (sacrament, sign, something visible).

When rightly used in religion, the word "mystery" describes not a puzzle or a problem to be solved, not even the limit of our understanding, but a visible reality that suggests the hidden presence of God.

We walk frequently along the edges of divine mystery. If we listen closely, as we live God's love, we hear secrets...and we tell secrets of the kingdom, of God's visitation. Our mission as Christians is, in fact, to tell secrets, to tell what we have seen and heard.

Your Faith, Your Life: An Invitation to the Episcopal Church, disguised as a reference book of information, is about transformation. It is about the lion in your heart becoming a lion in your world. It is about relationship. It is about process: being attentive, intelligent, reasonable, responsible, and in Love. It is about increasing our attentiveness and transforming our consciousness through reflection on our faith and life and on being in Love. Ultimately, it is about secrets of the heart, whispers within of the hidden presence of the real. It is about telling secrets of God's visitation.   *— Bill*

A little over twenty-five years ago, while Bill Lewellis was deep into ordained ministry, I was attending the first-ever Episcopal Youth Event held at the University of Illinois in Champaign–Urbana, in the summer of 1982. I was a sixteen-year-old member of Christ Episcopal Church in Poughkeepsie, New York. Bill and I might be divided by a generation, but we are joined together in our love for God, a commitment to spirituality and mission, and an attitude of approaching life as a journey of transformation — a journey of uncovering the dream that God has sown deep within us.

I love that story that Henry Nouwen tells of the lion waiting to be revealed within the marble. It is a story of a secret waiting to be told by the hands of an artist. As Bill reminds us, each of us also has a secret to tell. God has sown within each of us a dream, an image that reflects the love of Christ.

In an interview by Krista Tippett in *Speaking of Faith*, Rabbi Sandy Eisenberg Sasso tells of research indicating that by the age of five all children have "an innate spirituality, a great sense of wonder, spontaneity, imagination and creativity, and a connection to something larger than themselves." She goes on to say that many children lack the language to "give expression to that sense of something deeper."[1]

I have attended an Episcopal church since I was four years old, and I became a member of the Episcopal Church when I was baptized at eight. I grew up with the language of the Episcopal Church — a language of images, actions, words, and postures. It is a language layered with memories and meaning. But I am the minority. Most Episcopalians didn't grow up in the Episcopal Church. The language of the Episcopal Church, to some, seems like an untold secret — like a secret handshake of longstanding members of a private club. It is not meant to be a secret, but instead to reveal a mystery.

The language of the Episcopal Church need not be a secret. That's why I set out to write a book for teenagers, *My Faith, My Life*, and now this book with Bill. This book can be, however, only an introduction. Language, and indeed faith, are living; they gain meaning though use; they change with our ever deepening personal context. Each time you celebrate Eucharist with your community, the language of worship will gain a layer of meaning. Its meaning will change and so will you. That's what a spiritual journey is like. It transforms.

Throughout my life I have welcomed opportunities for new growth and insights, but until Bill shared with me how he has integrated the transcendental imperatives of Bernard Lonergan into his faith and life, I did not have a framework for seeing those insights as a process of transformation. We have adapted those imperatives — be attentive, be intelligent, be reasonable, be responsible, be in Love, and, if necessary, change — as the framework for *Your Faith, Your Life* so that, as you engage the information in the text, you might also journey toward ever-deepening personal transformation.

We never lose the opportunity to develop the language of spirituality, whether we are five, twenty-five, fifty-five, or one hundred and five. Planted deep within each of us, God's dream awaits to emerge just as the image of Aslan emerged from the artist's marble.   *—Jenifer*

---

1. Krista Tippett, "The Spirituality of Parenting," *Speaking of Faith* (St. Paul, Minn.: American Public Media, April 3, 2008).

HOW TO READ THIS BOOK

Your Faith, Your Life is more than an invitation to the Episcopal Church. It is an invitation to reflect on personal transformation as you consider facts about the Episcopal Church. Disguised as a reference book of information, as Bill has suggested, this book outlines a path toward authenticity and personal transformation.

Five imperatives frame the information: be attentive, be intelligent, be reasonable, be responsible, and be in Love. We present these in chapter 1. The imperatives, however, require an ingredient this book cannot provide — you, the reader. Your experiences, thoughts, beliefs, and very being provide the context that you bring to this text.

Reading the text of your life will provide crucial context for your faith. To invite you to begin a practice of reading your life and listening to what it says, each chapter in this book begins with a reflection by Bill from his life. Embodied in his stories is an invitation to you to remember yours. Bring his story into the chapter and begin to recall your own stories.

The chapter also contains specific opportunities to reflect on a saying or a question — both within and at the end of the chapter. The set of questions at the end of each chapter follows the framework of the five imperatives, beginning by inviting you to remember a particular moment in your life. Engage your story with the questions and the five imperatives as your process toward intellectual, moral, and religious conversion — in a word: transformation.

Terms appearing in *bold face* are defined in the glossary, beginning on page 189.

Chapter One

Transforming Questions

At the core of human life is a search for meaning. Nothing else truly satisfies. We need to know that our lives have meaning. Among theologian Paul Tillich's contributions to religious understanding was to insist that what we mean by God is actually that which is of ultimate meaning, that our search for meaning is ultimately a search for God.

When seeking information, there are no dumb questions. When seeking meaning, however, you may have had the experience of being led on a rabbit trail by someone's uninsightful questions. For in our search for meaning, even if we discover a right answer to an irrelevant question, seeking to answer that inappropriate question will take us way off course.

"If I had an hour to solve a problem and my life depended on the solution," Albert Einstein said, "I would spend the first fifty-five minutes determining the proper question to ask, for once I knew the proper question, I could solve the problem in less than five minutes."

Einstein understood the importance of asking the right question, the intelligent question, and the effective question. Seeking to discover the proper question has long been central to Bill's thinking, to his prayer, his faith, and his life. He was introduced to the priority of the appropriate question — how crucial it is to ask the right question — during the 1960s by Canadian Jesuit philosopher and theologian Bernard Lonergan, who cited four "transcendental imperatives" and their interrelated questions, to be asked with intentional awareness on one's path toward authenticity and integrity.

Authenticity, in the framework of this book, refers to our disciplined attempts to be attentive, intelligent, reasonable, and responsible and, therein, to be open to intellectual conversions of our minds, moral conversions of our wills, and religious conversions of our hearts. The journey begins where we are and seeks to get beyond ourselves to the unique and beloved persons God has created us to be. This journey to integrity, into the mystery of God's love for us, takes courage.

> Authenticity is a journey that begins where we are
> and seeks to get beyond ourselves to the unique and
> beloved persons God has created us to be.

Bill introduced these imperatives to Jenifer during conversations about what truths God was calling her to. She also found them to be consonant with her way of being in the world. We come to these questions differently — Bill as a theologian, father, husband, and son, and Jenifer as an economist, wife, mother, and daughter. But both of us share a love for the search: to know God, to know ourselves, to know our faith, and what all of that might mean for our lives. Likewise, you come with your own experiences and ways of being.

In his introduction to *Religious Literacy: What Every American Needs to Know — and Doesn't,* Stephen Prothero contends that "faith without under-standing is the standard [among Americans who] are both deeply religious and profoundly ignorant about religion. They are Protestants who can't name the four Gospels, Catholics who can't name the seven sacraments, and Jews who can't name the five books of Moses." Their faith, he continues, "is almost entirely devoid of content. One of the most religious countries on earth is also a nation of religious illiterates."

With that in mind, *Your Faith, Your Life* contains basic content, informa-tion for Episcopalians who want to deepen their knowledge of the Episcopal Church and for those who are considering making the Episcopal Church their church home. Beyond basic information, this book suggests a path for those who seek understanding of their faith and their life as well as transformation, deeper conversion, as they walk with God. Thus, the emphasis on the crucial importance of asking the right questions.

If you turn back to the table of contents, you'll find four main section headings: "Be," "Seeking the True," "Seeking the Good," "Seeking God," and five sub-headings: "Be Attentive," "Be Intelligent," "Be Reasonable," "Be Responsible," and "Be in Love."

As someone who has chosen to join a faith community, you are deepening your commitment to an intentional journey of discovery and transformation. This can be for you a journey of new experiences, deepening reflection, pene-trating insight, and conversion. Because your journey must be guided by good questions in order not to be derailed, the five imperatives will help you frame your questions.

Like the Episcopal understanding of being born again — again and again — personal transformation is an ongoing journey. It is a process of attentiveness

> As you read *Your Faith, Your Life,* ask questions. Open
> your mind and heart to God. Consider your own faith,
> your own life. To whom or what do you give your
> heart? How do you understand your relationship with
> God? When have you experienced moments of grace
> and transformation?

(being an attentive subject), understanding (being an intelligently inquiring subject), judgment (being a rationally reflective and reasonable subject), and decision (being a responsibly deliberating subject).

Stop reading frequently, to ask transforming questions. Ask questions while you explore the imperatives that guide your journey to integrity and transformation.

BE ATTENTIVE

Be attentive to your experience, to your senses, feelings, intuition, and imagination. Upon this evidence, you will form ideas, hunches that may be right or wrong. Later, what you think you understand will depend on what you have sensed or imagined, what you have paid attention to, or not. If you have been inattentive, you will be clueless. Oversights will eventually need to be corrected.

Paul Fromberg, a liturgist experienced in introducing new, and often ancient, liturgies suggests this way of being attentive: Instead of asking yourself (or your congregation after a newly experienced liturgy), "What did you think?" ask, "What did you see?" So often we bypass the step of noticing, being attentive with our senses. We skip to judgment. By beginning with our senses, we heighten our awareness, and open ourselves to new experiences with the intention of receiving them without judgment. By doing so, we broaden the possibility of gaining new insight.

A February 2004 *Wall Street Journal* special report on trends included this: "How do trend spotters find what they're looking for? They keep their eyes open." Be attentive.

This book will help you be attentive to this particular journey by introducing the language and practice of our worship, the stories of the Bible, the people and events of our church history, the creeds, and the structure of the Episcopal Church. Knowing the words of our faith will help you own your experiences and share them with others. As you read this book, as you journey with your community, be attentive.

BE INTELLIGENT

This second imperative asks you to inquire into the meaning of your experience, the data or information you have received. What does this mean? Experiencing something is different from understanding the meaning of your experience. Be intelligent as you interpret what you have seen, heard, or sensed. Have you missed any crucial information? How else might your experience be understood? Are there alternative explanations?

By separating experience from understanding you become aware of how your current understanding may shape what you see and hear. How does the lens through which you see the world affect your experience? Challenge yourself to see and hear with new eyes and ears. Sometimes a new experience may not accommodate your current understanding. When this happens, reexamine both your earlier and your new experience. Did you miss something? Does this new evidence challenge you to adjust your understanding?

BE REASONABLE

Insights occur spontaneously as well as after considered reflection on one's experience, but are they correct? There may be several ways, some even contradictory ways, to understand your experience. Determining which meaning rings most true requires reasonable judgment. Choose the meaning to which you are drawn and live with it for a while. Does it make sense in light of other experiences you have had? Does it make sense in light of the witness of history, culture, and the experiences of others?

> A helpful exercise is to consider stories from the Bible or the lives of saints with similar themes. How do they inform your understanding? What does your community say about the various possibilities? Be reasonable about what you believe.

This step of judging is different from both experience and insight. Ask yourself, have you judged wisely? Is this your best interpretation of the data? Remain open to new possibilities. God is with you, bringing new things to life in you.

BE RESPONSIBLE

Having judged what you consider to be true, based on your experience and reflection on your experience, you now face the question, "What am I going to do about it?" Thus the fourth imperative: *Be responsible* in what you do with what you have judged to be true. Is the action you are considering truly worthwhile? What commitments will you make, what risks will you take, to act responsibly?

The four transcendental imperatives are: be attentive, be intelligent, be reasonable, and be responsible— transcendental because they are equally valid for *everyone, everywhere,* and *always*; imperatives because you continually work at them.

This will come into play especially in chapter 7 of this book about what God is calling you to do. Discerning God's will is something we do each day with even the smallest choices, such as what to eat, say, and do. We also discern God's will when faced with life-changing experiences such as falling in love. Be responsible in deciding what to do as a result of what you have judged to be true and the correct understanding of your experience.

THREEFOLD CONVERSION WHILE SEEKING THE TRUE, THE GOOD, AND GOD

Look again at the section headings in the table of contents. "Seeking the true" involves being attentive, intelligent, and reasonable. "Seeking the good" involves being responsible. "Seeking God" involves being in love in an un-restricted way as God's love floods your heart. All involve an intentional dwelling with questions meant to transform the seeker. We invite you to use the four imperatives in the continuing development of your faith and the integrity of your life.

As a theologian as well as a philosopher, Lonergan added a fifth imperative. "Be in Love transformed." Be in God. Be in the relationship God offers you as revealed in your experience, in what you have discerned to be true and in what you have decided to do. Being in love means being open to transformation in God, self-transcendence, visualizing yourself in an open-handed, palms-turned-up position of prayer, being open to the Mystery that grounds your being. This fifth imperative, then, brings you back to experience, understand, judge, and decide, again and again, with renewed integrity, open to multiple conversions, as you move along the way toward personal authenticity and self-transcendence. We invite you, then, as you read this book: *Be attentive. Be intelligent. Be reasonable. Be responsible. Be in Love. And, if necessary, change.*

"If necessary," of course, is rhetorical. We always need to change; we always need to strive for integrity, to be born again and again, to be changed from the inside out, to be transformed by good news, to be in Love transformed.

Openness to threefold conversion is crucial as you ask yourself the questions prompted by each imperative. Being *attentive, intelligent, and reasonable* opens you to intellectual conversion. Being *responsible*, shifting from seeking the true to seeking the good, opens you to moral conversion. Being *in Love* opens you to religious conversion. There, life begins anew, where a new self is to be understood, only to be transcended. Born again, we attend again to our experience, insight, judgment, and decision, to a rumor of angels promising deeper intellectual and moral, and religious conversion.

Though no one of us arrives completely in this life, the good news, best said by St. Augustine, is: "Thou [God] hast formed us for Thyself, and our hearts are restless till they find rest in Thee." Indeed, we are people of "the way," seeking the depths of Love.

We live in a world of constant change. Some of us are not comfortable with that. If you are not so comfortable with change as you might like to be, try to spiritualize the experience by considering changes that affect your life as opportunities for intellectual, moral, or religious conversion. The key, as you consider potentially transforming questions while reading this book, is sustained critical attentiveness to these four levels of how we come to know ourselves, the world around us, and God — experience, understanding, judgment, and decision — and an openness to multiple intellectual, moral, and religious conversions.

"A person is becoming authentic who is consistent in the struggle to be attentive, intelligent, reasonable, and responsible," according to Lonergan. "This precarious and ever-developing state depends on long and sustained faithfulness to the transcendental precepts."[2]

A person doesn't have to be religious to achieve authenticity, though one does need to be authentic to be truly religious. You don't have to be liberal or conservative. Your reading of the Bible may tend toward the literal or you may take it as metaphor, rich holy writ given for your conversion. You don't have to profess adherence to the teachings of any man or woman or institution. You don't have to be a Democrat or a Republican. You don't have

---

2. Bernard Lonergan, "Dialectic of Authority," *A Third Collection: Papers by Bernard Lonergan,* ed. Fred Crowe (New York: Paulist Press, 1985), 8.

to be Roman Catholic, Episcopalian, Lutheran, Moravian, Methodist, Jewish, Muslim, or Buddhist. You don't have to be "right," but you do need to be open to conversion. If necessary, change.

BEING IN LOVE

In Love, of course, means in God's love. The first great commandment as told in Matthew 22 is "You shall love the Lord your God with all your heart, and with all your soul, and with all your mind" (22:37). Matthew continues, "And the second is like it: 'You shall love your neighbor as yourself'" (22:39). In our love of neighbor we recognize God unformed, disguised in our world, like the lion in the block of marble.

Yes, it is possible in this life to love one's neighbor while paying no mind to God. Is it conceivable, however, for someone to love God and not love one's neighbor? Perhaps the answer to this question resides in the words, "And the second is like it."

We do not know God directly. Our families, the Jewish and Christian scriptures, Jesus, church, culture, friends, icons, images, and communication technologies (including the Internet, television, movies, newspapers, novels, music) have this in common. They are media — lenses and filters through which and whom come the visions and values and meaning we live by. They do not come directly from God. They are mediated through our experience.

For St. Paul, Jesus Christ is Mediator par excellence. "For there is one God; there is also one mediator between God and humankind, Christ Jesus" (1 Tim. 2:5), and "Long ago God spoke to our ancestors in many and various ways by the prophets, but in these last days he has spoken to us by a Son. . . . He is the reflection of God's glory and the exact imprint of God's very being" (Hebrews 1:1–3).

And Jesus tells us that if we know him we will know the Father (John 14:1–14), that we are to love one another as he has loved us and by our love for one another we will be known as his disciples (John 13:34–35), that whatever we do to our sisters and brothers in need we do to him (Matthew 25:31–46), and that he will be with his disciples to the end of the age (Matthew 28:20).

Inside the gates of heaven, imagine coming upon a fork in the road where there are two signs. One sign points northwest "for those who love God." The other sign points northeast, the way "for those who love their neighbor." That may be the only case where the saying attributed to Yogi Berra works: "If you come to a fork in the road, take it." For, like the two great commandments, the roads converge.

Our hope for this book is that it might be for you a deeply spiritual roadmap. Take the imperatives into your head and your heart, adapting them to the rhythm of your own consciousness in ways that you may find yourself in Love — intellectually, morally, and religiously transformed — discovering, again and again, increased authenticity and integrity in your faith and your life, discerning ever more clearly God's call to be.

✠ TRANSFORMING QUESTIONS

1. **Be Attentive:** Remember the first time that you came to this particular church. What did you notice? What was the event? Who was present?

2. **Be Intelligent:** What does what you noticed say about the community?

3. **Be Reasonable:** What does the community say about itself? (You might want to look at the church's mission statement.) How does what the community says about itself compare with your experience?

4. **Be Responsible:** What about the community's mission appeals to you? How might you contribute to that mission?

5. **Be in Love Transformed:** What must you give up to commit yourself to that ministry? What promise does that sacrifice offer?

Chapter Two

Beginnings

BE

Josef Fuchs, a German Jesuit who taught at the Gregorian University in Rome during the 1960s, informed my first experience of Christian moral theology. It was not what I was expecting. I was expecting to study the law. God's law, church law, case studies, morality, and legality. Answers.

I was primed for answers. Clear and sure answers. Rules for life. Several years before, I had begun collecting answers. On 3 x 5 index cards.

On an upper corner of each card, I wrote topical words and phrases, questions for which people wanted answers. From my reading during college seminary days, I'd make notes on the cards. Pearls. The Catholic's ready answer. Answers for life. For my ministry as a priest.

Only once did I question my system. Three-by-five cards did not accommodate complexity well. I recognized that I needed to upgrade my system. I began to use 5 x 7 cards. It's not easy to get beyond linear thinking.

Armed with 5 x 7 index cards from America, I was ready to outline clear answers from Father Fuchs's moral theology class.

During the first few weeks of class, however, he read and talked about passages from St. Paul's letters. "Hello," I thought. Was this the moral theology class? There's someone here reading from the Bible. So at odds with my expectations for the course — I was expecting a journey through the law and moral dilemmas — Josef Fuchs walked through the letters of St. Paul, especially through those places where Paul says we have been changed, transformed, reborn. In Christ.

He suggested again and again that in that change, in that transformation, in that rebirth — in Christ — we discover the defining moment for Christian living: that the answer to "What must I do?" is contained in the question, "Who am I?" — an early version of WWJD? — and that the Christian moral imperative is rooted not in law but in Jesus Christ and in the person I have become in Christ. Paul soon follows "You are a new creation," Josef Fuchs pointed out, with "Therefore, *be* (who you are)!" This sequence, Fuchs said, was Paul's moral theology." You *are* a new creation in Christ. You are mystery. Let the mystery unfold. Let the secret be told. Be reconciled. Be glad. Be thankful. Be compassionate. Be who you are. Be that new creation in Christ.

That, he suggested, was the heart of Christian morality: Jesus Christ and the new creation we have become in Christ. Josef Fuchs called it the Pauline Indicative-Imperative: You *are* a new creation in Christ. In Christ, you *are* raised. Therefore, *be*....

It's crucial that we recognize the priority of the Indicative, because Christians are called to the impossible, to a life where the impossible becomes mandatory. This can lead to frustration and despair if we reverse the order, putting the imperative before the indicative. First, we *are* in Christ. First, we *are* a new creation in Christ. That has to be first. Then, only then, can we *be* or *do*. The Pauline Indicative-Imperative remains the basis for the priority of prayer and worship in our lives.

Around the same time Father Fuchs invited me into the Pauline Indicative-Imperative, a classmate introduced me to the joy and wonder that in mystery and sacrament — in our community celebration of Eucharist — we get in touch with new creation in Christ and begin to become transformed in Christ. In the eucharistic mystery, we discover, stumble upon, get enveloped by, allow ourselves to be immersed in the mystery we are meant somehow to be and tell.

I tore up my index cards.   *— B.L.*

◆　◆　◆

WATERS OF CREATION

The mystery of life first began on earth long ago in what scientists call "deep time." Nearly three billion years ago, cellular life began in shallow oceans. Two billion years later life had progressed into multi-celled animals visible to the naked eye. Eventually life forms developed that could survive on land. Life originated from the water, and life on land still needs water to survive.

People have long recognized the necessity of water in their stories of the beginnings of life. As Christians we share the creation story told by the Hebrews in which God breathed over the face of the waters to call forth all creation. From the waters, dry land appeared. From the waters, God called swarms of living creatures into being.

Water continued to play a central part in the journeys of the Hebrew people. God led the Hebrews through the waters of the Red Sea out of Egypt and slavery. God provided water for their journey in the desert wilderness. God led the people through the River Jordan into the Promised Land of Canaan. We read these stories in the Jewish scriptures (also called the Old Testament).

WATERS OF JESUS' BAPTISM

The Gospels of the Christian scriptures (also called the New Testament) tell another story of a watery beginning — the baptism of Jesus. Jesus' baptism began his ministry in the world. At Jesus' baptism in the Jordan River the heavens parted, the Spirit came down on Jesus, and God said, "You are my Son, the Beloved; with you I am well pleased" (Mark 1:11). In the ripples on the river, Jesus heard God calling him to be the suffering servant of the book of Isaiah. He struggled with God's "You are...." He was tempted in the desert to deny God's call. Ultimately, he went to his hometown synagogue in Nazareth, where he affirmed that, indeed, the Spirit of the Lord was upon him "to bring good news to the poor...to proclaim release to the captives and recovery of sight to the blind, to let the oppressed go free..." (Luke 4). Jesus said, "Yes, I am." Consider the waters of your own baptism where God said "You are...." Consider the ripples on the water of your own joy and wonder, your struggle, your transformation, your "Yes, I am." This is the heart of Christian moral theology that Bill speaks about in the introductory essay to this chapter — be.

> Through baptism, we are made a new creation in Christ. It is after this mystery that we can begin to be transformed and be who we are.

WATERS OF BIRTH AND REBIRTH

Each of us was conceived in a place rich in water. For nine months we floated in a sea of water inside our mother's womb — first as one cell, then two, then four, then eight. Soon we developed organs and limbs. Finally, one day, we broke through those waters and into the world.

On the day of your baptism, you were born yet again, this time into the body of Christ, the church. Again you burst forth from water as a new person. Even if you do not remember your own baptism, you've likely seen other people being baptized.

Back on your special day, a priest poured water over your head, or completely plunged you into the water. Now, you didn't reenter your mother's womb, as a man named Nicodemus wondered when he heard Jesus talking about being born again (John 3:1–10). But you were born again. You can even think of the baptismal font, the basin that holds the waters of baptism, as a womb from which you were born again. On the day you were baptized, the

Holy Spirit moved in those waters, making you a new person and giving you spiritual gifts for your life.

Water is a central symbol of baptism.

The waters of baptism are powerful. They are the same waters of *creation* over which God breathed and called forth life. They are the same waters of *freedom* through which God led the Hebrews out of a life of slavery in Egypt and the waters of *promise* through which they walked into new life. They are the same waters in which *Jesus* was baptized and the same living water that Jesus offered the Samaritan woman at the well. In these powerful and living waters you were reborn. By those waters you share in the waters of creation, liberation, promise, and new life in Christ. In the waters of baptism you were bathed in the living water where you will never thirst again.

Today's baptisms, unlike the baptisms in the muddy Jordan River, can be overly sentimental. Babies dressed in white. Receptions with cake and ice cream. Baptisms truly are a cause for celebration, but in the festivities we may not notice that a big change is happening before our very eyes. Looking at early Christian baptismal rituals might help us better recognize the change.

Baptism in the Early Church

Baptism meant huge changes in the lives of early Christians. Becoming a Christian sometimes meant putting your very life in jeopardy. You would have to disobey Roman laws that required you to make sacrifices to the Roman gods, which could have easily gotten you arrested, tried, and even put to death. Some newly baptized Christians, such as those in the army, had to give up their jobs. Becoming a Christian in the early centuries after Christ literally meant turning toward a new way of living.

Catechumens began the ritual of baptism by facing West, the direction of the setting sun and the symbolic direction of darkness and evil. They stood on a hair shirt to indicate that they desired to die to their life of sin, then renounced evil three times, professing their desire to give up — virtually die to — their old way of life.

The catechumens then turned to the East, the direction of the rising of the sun and the symbolic place of new life and three times professed their faith in Christ. Then they stepped into a pool of water, submersing their entire bodies. This pool of water symbolized a tomb in which their old selves died and their sins were washed away. It also represented a mother's womb, out of which a new person was born. Finally, stepping out of the water, they were clothed in a white garment that symbolized their new life in Christ.

The white alb that bishops, priests, and deacons wear during Holy Eucharist and other church services reminds us of the white dress of baptism.

While we live in a country that does not persecute Christians, living as a Christian still means that we see the world differently than others do. So just like early Christians we are expected to act differently than others around us. We see a world in which God loves all of creation and hopes for a world in which people act in ways that show that they love themselves, one another, and all creation. As new creations in Christ, we are asked to collaborate with God's loving purpose by loving our neighbors, striving for justice, respecting the dignity of every human being. Just as it was for early Christians, your baptism was the beginning of a new life.

Your Baptism

Your baptism likely took place years ago, long before you could speak or understand what was going on. You might want to take some time to search for your baptismal record or photographs of the day of your baptism. Your baptismal certificate will tell you the date of your baptism, the name of the priest who baptized you, and the names of your godparents. If your parents, godparents, or others who attended your baptism are still living, ask them to share stories and photographs of the day.

On that day, your parents and godparents presented you to God and the world. They brought you into the **Baptismal Covenant** by making promises on your behalf to believe in God and to follow Christ. They promised to bring you up in the Christian faith. (Chapter 10 on sacraments explores the Baptismal Covenant in greater detail.)

Our baptism is a gift from God. Faith changes how we see the world. The lens of faith in Jesus Christ lets us see the world differently. Instead of a world of random events, we see a world that is part of God's purpose. Instead of a world of unrelated individuals, we see a world of individuals called to be in relationship with God and one another. Instead of a world with an indifferent creator, we see a Creator in love with and intimately concerned with creation. You can choose to accept or reject that gift. Reading this book and engaging your knowledge and experience of God within the framework of the five imperatives — be attentive, be intelligent, be reasonable, be responsible, and be in love — will help make that choice.

COVENANT

We've used the word "covenant" a few times in this chapter. It's a word we don't hear much today. A **covenant** is a relationship freely entered into by two parties who promise to be faithful to each other. God initiates the relationship and promises to transform those who respond in faith.

A covenant is different from a contract. Although people make promises in a contract and do so freely, contracts are meant to align the interests of the parties involved, not to transform anyone. An example of a contract is signing an agreement to buy a home. The sellers want to get as much for the house as possible. The buyers want to pay as little as possible. A contract arrives at a price where the buyer's and seller's interests are aligned. The contract facilitates a transaction that fulfills the interests of both parties.

The Baptismal Covenant is the basis for our relationship with God through Christ and God's gift to us. We respond with a series of promises. The Baptismal Covenant is on page 304 of the Book of Common Prayer.

Being in a covenant transforms you. God offers us a covenant that we might be God's people. God promises to be faithful. By accepting God's promises we are changed. We see the world through new eyes, through the lens of the covenant. Instead of seeing the world as indifferent, random, hostile, and threatening, life is purposeful, relational, and inviting. God's covenant shapes our every action and is forever.

Covenant and the Jewish Scriptures

God enters into a relationship with people in the form of a covenant. We learn in the Jewish scriptures (Old Testament) that God promised that the Hebrews would be his people and he would be their God. God required them to be faithful, to do justice, to love mercy, and to walk humbly with their God (Micah 6:8). God established a number of covenants — one with Noah, another with Abraham, and another with Moses.

As Christians we share in God's covenant and in God's saving acts told from several perspectives and with many twists and turns in the Jewish scriptures. The God of Israel, our God, freed the Hebrews from slavery in Egypt and led them to the promised land of Canaan. The map below shows one route they may have taken from northern Egypt through the Sinai Peninsula and into present-day Israel/Palestine and Jordan. God remained with them

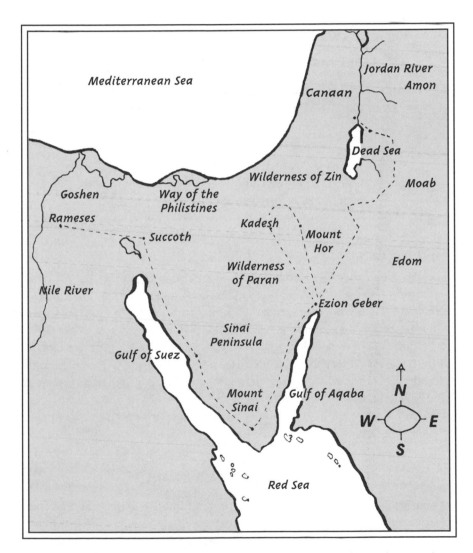

The dotted line on this map of the Ancient Near East shows one way the Israelites may have traveled from slavery in Egypt (far left) to the Promised Land in Canaan (far right).

through forty years of wandering in the wilderness and provided for their needs just as God remains with us today and gives us what we need. God is faithful. God is faithful to the covenant and is with us always.

Covenant and the Christian Scriptures

Our God is the God who sent his only son, Jesus, to live and die as one of us. Through Jesus, God renewed his covenant and offered it to all people. In the Christian scriptures (New Testament) at Jesus' last Passover meal, Jesus gave us a **New Covenant**. During the Eucharist every Sunday we remember his words: "Drink from it, all of you; for this is my blood of the covenant, which is poured out for many for the forgiveness of sins" (Matthew 26:27–28). In this new covenant Jesus promises to bring us into the kingdom of God. We respond to the new covenant by loving one another as Jesus loves us.

The New Covenant is a new relationship with God through Jesus Christ. This New Covenant was prophesied in Jeremiah 31.

Baptismal Covenant

The covenant given by God in the Jewish scriptures and in the Christian scriptures — and our Baptismal Covenant — all share the same basic characteristics: we freely enter, we make promises, and we are changed by God. If you were baptized as an infant, you might say that you did not freely choose to be baptized. You would be right. For you, baptism was a gift, just as being born was a gift. Your parents wanted you to be part of the Christian community, the body of Christ. So they chose for you to be baptized. They spoke on your behalf and promised to teach you about Jesus Christ and what it means to live a Christian life. They stood up in front of family and friends and made it clear that they wanted you to be Christ's own forever!

REAFFIRMING THE COVENANT

When you are confirmed, received, or reaffirm the Baptismal Covenant you are choosing to renew a covenant with God — to confirm your baptismal promises and seek God's strength to live into that covenant. During every baptism, confirmation, or reaffirmation, the gathered members of the congregation renew their own Baptismal Covenant.

By looking at the service of confirmation, reception, and reaffirmation of baptismal vows, you can see exactly what you are committing yourself to. Let's look at the service.

Presentation and Examination

After you are presented, the bishop asks you two questions:

- Do you reaffirm your renunciation of evil?

- Do you renew your commitment to Jesus Christ?

Responding with "I do" means you want to turn away from sin and darkness and toward life in Christ. You are saying that you are turning from the *values* of sin and death to the *values* of God and life. Instead of acting in ways that deny God and break relationships with others, you are saying your actions will honor God and nurture relationships with others.

The two questions the bishop asks candidates for confirmation, reception, and reaffirmation mirror the six questions asked at baptism. Look on page 302 of the Book of Common Prayer to read those six questions.

The Ten Commandments give us a guideline for right and wrong actions: "Remember the Sabbath day" and "Honor your father and your mother" are two examples (Exodus 20). Jesus provided a summary of the law with this commandment: love God and love your neighbor as yourself (Matthew 22:35–40). You are promising that your actions will follow God's desire for you. How do we know God's desire? God's desire will be consistent with the Ten Commandments and the summary of the law. God's desires bring life to you, to others, and to your relationships.

Renewing the Promises

Once you have expressed your commitment to follow Christ, the priest continues by asking:

- Do you believe in God the Father?

- Do you believe in Jesus Christ, the Son of God?

- Do you believe in God the Holy Spirit?

Those questions refer to the Apostles' Creed. In chapter 5 of this book we explore the Apostles' Creed carefully.

The word "creed" comes from the Latin word *credere,* which has the same root as the word "heart." Saying "I believe" isn't just an abstract statement about whether we believe God exists. It's a statement about where our heart is and who will guide our everyday choices. When we proclaim "I believe" we are saying we are giving our hearts to God, and to give our hearts to God changes how we choose to live.

One way to think about the Apostles' Creed is as a recitation of what God has done for us — creating heaven and earth, living among us, dying and conquering death, and dwelling among and with us today. In the Baptismal Covenant, the questions that follow, then, prompt our response, our **baptismal promises**:

- Will you continue in the apostles' teaching and fellowship, in the breaking of bread, and in the prayers?

- Will you persevere in resisting evil, and, whenever you fall into sin, repent and return to the Lord?

- Will you proclaim by word and example the good news of God in Christ?

- Will you seek and serve Christ in all persons, loving your neighbor as yourself?

- Will you strive for justice and peace among all people, and respect the dignity of every human being?

When you answer, "I will, with God's help," to each of these questions, you are promising to take very specific actions throughout your life. You are promising to worship regularly, to resist evil, and to ask for forgiveness when you do not live up to your promises. You are promising to talk to others about God's love. You are promising to love your neighbor as yourself and to strive for justice and peace. Fulfilling these promises is what it means to live into the Baptismal Covenant.

Prayers and Blessings

After you have renewed your Baptismal Covenant, the entire congregation prays to God to give you the strength to fulfill your promises. They ask God to deliver you from sin, open your heart with grace and truth, fill you with the Spirit, keep you in faith, and teach you to love others. They ask God to send you out into the world to do the good work you have promised to do. Faith, after all, is a relationship with God that we act out in community.

The congregation is present on that day and beyond to help you keep your promises, to stand with you in tough times, to celebrate with you in happy times, and to encourage you to take your faith out into the world.

After the prayers, the bishop lays his hand on you and blesses you, asking God to strengthen you with the Holy Spirit, empower you for God's service, and sustain you all the days of your life. If you are being received, the bishop "recognizes you as a member of the one holy catholic and apostolic church" (Book of Common Prayer, page 310). And, if you are reaffirming your baptismal promises, the bishop asks the Holy Spirit to "direct and uphold you in the service of Christ and his kingdom."

The bishop represents the teaching and community of the apostles from the time of Jesus all the way to today and that fellowship throughout the world today. The laying on of hands is the symbolic act that visibly connects you to the apostles and the universal church.

CHOOSING TO PROCLAIM YOUR LOVE FOR GOD

Confirmation, reception, and reaffirmation are opportunities to publicly state your love for God and your desire to live into God's promises for you. It is an affirmation of faith that demonstrates a renewed commitment to Christ. If you choose to renew your commitment, you are the one who answers, "I do," "I believe," and "I will, with God's help."

Saying "I believe in God" is our heart responding to God's love. Marjorie Thompson says it this way: "God's desire for us ignites the spark of our desire for God."[3]

God has given us the ability to make the choice to respond to God's covenant freely. Whether you choose to respond or not, you will always be a member of God's household. You were made a member of the household of God at baptism and you will forever bear the mark of Christ.

This book will help you understand what these questions mean, guide you about how to keep those promises, and help you decide: Do I turn from evil and toward Jesus? Do I believe in the Trinity? Do I promise to act in the way that follows Jesus? These promises form the backbone of our faith and our relationship with God.

---

3. Marjorie Thompson, *Soul Feast* (Louisville: Westminster John Knox Press, 2005), 33.

MADE IN THE IMAGE OF GOD
AND MARKED AS CHRIST'S OWN FOREVER

If you read the questions that you will be asked carefully, you might wonder whether you can, in all honesty, say yes to them. Don't worry. Questioning whether you can promise such faithfulness means you're taking these questions seriously and being honest with yourself. Like all people, you will fall short of fulfilling your promises. The Bible is filled with people who fall short and struggle with God — from Jacob who wrestled with God in his dreams and Jonah who tried to run away from God in the Jewish scriptures, to Peter, the apostle who denied Jesus three times in the Christian scriptures. God wants us to offer our whole selves — our faith and doubt, our strength and weakness, and our joy and pain. God asks for nothing less. And as theologian Bernard Lonergan reminds us, we are on a path of continual conversion toward authenticity. Life in Christ is not about arriving.

You Have God

Luckily for us, we aren't alone when we are faced with choices to fulfill our baptismal promises. We have God, Christ, and one another. Look closely at the response to each question. The answer is "I will, *with God's help.*" God is with you. God has been with you since the beginning and will always be with you to give you the strength to make good choices.

You have God, Christ, and community.

God has given each of us the gifts we need to live a good life. This shouldn't surprise us. From birth we bear the image of God. Genesis tells us that God said, "Let us make humankind in our image according to our likeness" (Genesis 1:26). People often remark at the likeness of a newborn baby to its parents. "She has her father's eyes," or "He has his mother's nose." Our genetic makeup reflects the DNA of our mother and father. In the same way we also reflect the image of our Creator, God.

Simply put, like God, we are made to love and to create. We have the abilities to heal broken relationships, to do justice, to provide for the physical and mental well-being of others, and even to create new life — both physically by creating new families and spiritually by sharing our faith with others. God has given us the ability to live into our baptismal promises.

Now, it would be unrealistic or naïve to end the conversation there. Yes, we are made to do good, but we sometimes choose to do bad things. We ignore God and think only of ourselves. We forget the goodness of God that is in us. We harm ourselves and others. We fall short of our promises. It's a given.

You Have Christ

Knowing that we will fall short of the mark, one of the promises we make is that *whenever* we fall into sin, we will repent and return to the Lord. Notice that we don't say *if* we fall into sin. Falling into sin is inevitable. But even before that happens, God forgives us and sets our hearts right again and again. What we promise to do is to ask for God's forgiveness and guidance.

God loved us so much that he became one of us. Jesus, God's only Son, out of love, gave himself up for us on the cross. God raised him from the dead. We share in Jesus' resurrection and in new life offered through Christ. In the waters of baptism we became a new creation in Christ. Our foreheads were marked with the sign of the cross. We were sealed by the Holy Spirit and marked as Christ's own forever.

You Have Community

Your community — the rest of the church, household of God — will help you keep your promises. Belief in God is not a private matter. The entire congregation witnesses the promises you make and they promise in turn to do all in their power to support you in your life in Christ. These are the people with whom you worship, study, pray, and serve. These are the people with whom you say the Nicene Creed each Sunday. When your belief falters, others will believe for you.

In the Episcopal Church baptism, confirmation, reception, and reaffirmation are public events. They transform the individual and the community. The community walks the journey together.

HOW WILL READING THIS BOOK HELP?

Preparing to renew your baptismal promises is an opportunity to learn about what it means to follow Jesus Christ, to believe in a triune God — God as Father, Son, and Holy Spirit — and to live according to our baptismal promises. This book was written to help you explore these beliefs and promises.

If you are to claim your faith, you must actively seek to understand God, yourself, and your relationship with God. This book will help you learn about Jesus and God, the language of worship, belief, church structure, and sacraments so that you can share your belief and practices with others and participate in the planning of worship at your own church. You will explore how to read and think about the Bible so that you can hear what God is saying today. You will learn about prayer so that you can deepen your relationship with God. You will learn about ministry (a call each of us receives from God to serve) and discover methods to discern your own ministry.

We invite you to a process of transformation by being attentive to what you are reading and open your heart to the witness of what you are reading to the Bible, to the Book of Common Prayer, and to your own experiences. The Bible tells about God, Jesus, and ourselves. The Book of Common Prayer defines our worship as a community. Our experiences as a community are where God meets us and is revealed.

Each chapter has questions that will engage with the five imperatives to consider your reading and experience. Talk about them together. They are a way to share your journey with people who care about you. Telling stories is essential to knowing ourselves as sons and daughters of God and proclaiming God to others.

Your church community will support you in your inquiry. Take advantage of the wealth of their experience and knowledge. Often other people can reveal a different perspective of God.

You've probably already noticed comments set off by rules from the main text. These comments will help guide your reading. Sometimes church vocabulary can be hard to understand. Don't let the words get in the way. The rich images, rituals, and words that express our understanding of God and the world are sometimes necessarily complex. God is ultimately a mystery, beyond knowing. Still, we use our senses — sight, touch, hearing, taste, and smell — to express that mystery. Any one way falls a little bit short because God is in all things and beyond our capacity to describe. Ultimately we may agree with the thirteenth-century monk Meister Eckhart, who said, "Nothing is so like God as silence."

CONCLUSION

Being a Christian is a journey of transformation that never ends. God continually yearns to be close to us, to be in a restored relationship with all people. Whether you seek to be baptized, to be confirmed, to be received, or to reaffirm your promises, you will be making a public affirmation of your faith and committing yourself to the specific promises. During the service we say "Yes" to God — to God's yearning for us and making a difference in our lives.

We hope that reading this book will help you continue your journey with God and membership in the church.

✝ TRANSFORMING QUESTIONS

1. **Be Attentive:** Consider the most recent baptism that you witnessed. What did you notice about the baptism? What did you see? What did you hear? What did the one baptized, the priest, parents, godparents, and congregation say and do?

2. **Be Intelligent:** What were you thinking and feeling at the time? What does your answer to this and the first question suggest about what baptism means?

3. **Be Reasonable:** Read the account of Jesus' baptism in Luke 1:21–22. What do you notice about Jesus' baptism? (Reading the passages before and after may help.) How does Jesus' baptism as told in Luke challenge or affirm what you believe about the role of baptism today?

4. **Be Responsible:** What might you do differently as a result of the insights you have gained about baptism?

5. **Be in Love Transformed:** What does your experience with baptism suggest about how you can remain open to personal conversion?

Chapter Three

Bible Stories

I WONDER

"**W**here can I find a Bible?" a woman asks. In an old cartoon from the *New Yorker,* the bookstore clerk tells her to look under self-help. That many Christians might not see the humor in the cartoon is not good news.

The Bible seems not to have a definite place in postmodern culture; many have trouble knowing what to make of it. Biblical literalists have added to the confusion. For the Bible is neither self-help, nor a rulebook, nor God's answers to moral questions, and certainly not a weapon with which to put others down.

The Bible is about God, not about us. People like you and me, inspired but still like us, wrote it to tell how they experienced God. "God is like this for me," they say, or "This is how I experienced God," or "This is how the Risen Christ came into my life, as a gardener, a stranger on the road, a trusted friend, a visitor on the shore. He cooked breakfast for us. He broke bread with us." Their stories are meant for wonder.

A key moment in the Catechesis of the Good Shepherd, an approach to the religious formation of children rooted in the Bible, liturgy, and Montessori principles, is when the teacher, after telling a story from the Bible, looks into the eyes of the children, respecting each as persons, and says simply: *"I wonder*...why does Jesus love the sheep...why did the shepherd leave the ninety-nine to find the one that was lost...*I wonder*...what Andrew thought when Jesus said 'Follow me'...*I wonder*...does Jesus say that also to me...*I wonder*...what does that mean?"

Our scriptures, especially the Gospels we have accepted as normative for life, are radically challenging writings. For God is always out in front of us, calling us to be our best selves. The Gospels may be the most radical writings we could ever read if, indeed, we read them as a soul-searching, open-hearted, open-minded spiritual discipline. Despite perennial efforts to domesticate and tame God, the God of Jesus Christ makes the most liberal among us seem reactionary.

One thing that clearly signals that the Gospels were meant to challenge rather than to provide specific solutions to life's dilemmas, for example, is the tension that appears throughout the Gospel according to Luke between poverty and possessions, between the renunciation of possessions on the one hand and the equally demanding emphasis upon using our possessions to help others.

It is difficult to clear a path between the challenges of personal renunciation and proper use. The two perspectives — complete abandonment on the one hand and using possessions wisely on the other, neatly interwoven in the Gospel according to Luke — indicate that it is wise to be wary of one-verse Christianity. God does, indeed, use many media of self-disclosure.

It helps me when reading God's word to think of Nicodemus, who thought he had things pretty much together. He came to Jesus looking for an answer. Jesus proposed a question. Nicodemus came to hear a new thought. Jesus suggested a new way of thinking. Nicodemus walked.

I have a rubber stamp that says, "The Episcopal Church: Resisting simplistic theology since 1785." We resist simplistic theology by doing our soul searching not only with the Bible, not only with tradition, not only with our God-given reason and life experience, but with all three: testing each one with the other two. You may have heard that referred to as the Anglican three-legged stool: scripture, tradition, and reason combined with life experience.

God's word comes in image ("The kingdom of God is like . . . ") and commission ("Go and make disciples . . . ") and mystery ("Unless you are born from above") and question ("Who do you say that I am?"). It is more about personal response ("Here am I, send me") than about hard and quick answers.

On the one hand, the Bible is the word of God; on the other hand, only Jesus is God's Word. For Christians — obviously this would not be so for Jews, for Muslims, for Buddhists, or for other non-Christian believers in God — God's most focused, God's clearest self-disclosure is not the Bible but Jesus Christ, whose cross is a window into God's love, God's mercy, God's compassion, God's forgiveness.

God's word always comes to us in the flesh. Reading the Bible can be a walk with Nicodemus or a walk with Jesus.   *—B.L.*

◆ ◆ ◆

A WALK WITH JESUS AND GOD

We invite you, then, to walk with Jesus and to see your walk as part of the walk told in the Bible. The Bible is a collection of stories, songs, and prayers for and about special gatherings, important events, and family trips. It tells us something about who we are as people of God. The primary characters are God and God's people. The **Bible** tells of God's creative and redeeming actions throughout history. Through the stories we see threads of common traditions, identities, and cycles of creation, sin, redemption, and restoration.

The Jewish scriptures (the Hebrew Bible, the Old Testament) teach us about God and God's relationship with God's chosen people. God initiates this relationship with a covenant in which God promises to guide, provide, and love. In turn the Israelites promise to worship the One God and live by God's laws. The Jewish scriptures are made up of stories, laws, poetry, and history about God's steadfast love. The Christian scriptures continue the story of God's love and covenant. They tell of God coming into the world as a person, Jesus, who shows us the way of eternal life by his ministry, and who shows us what it means to love God, ourselves, and our neighbor. God entered our history as a human to deliver us from whatever separates us from God.

 We never finish reading the Bible. Each time we return to the Bible — we don't just remember; we learn more about ourselves and about our walk with God.

A LIBRARY OF BOOKS

The word "bible" comes from a Greek word meaning books. Think library. Although bound into a single volume, the Bible really isn't a single book, but a library of sixty-six books: twenty-seven books of the Christian scriptures and thirty-nine books of Jewish scriptures. In addition to these, the Roman Catholic and the Episcopal churches include writings designated by some as apocryphal, that is, not included in the authoritative standard. Recognizing that the Bible is a library helps us notice the variety of literature and time periods included in the Bible. It also suggests how to read it. First of all, just as we don't take the first book off the shelf in a library, we don't begin reading the Bible with page one and continue to the end. Generally, we choose a book from among many books based on what we're interested in or what question we want to explore. Second, just as a library contains many kinds of books, the books of the Bible are also examples of many types of literature. The Bible includes histories, sermons, legal documents, poetry, hymns, romances, stories of intrigue, and letters. Because each is written for a different purpose, we read them differently.

THE JEWISH AND CHRISTIAN SCRIPTURES

The Bible has two major parts — the Jewish scriptures (Old Testament) and the Christian scriptures (New Testament). But "testament" isn't a very accurate word. Although Old and New Testaments do *testify* to, or show, the way God has saved the people throughout history, the word "testament" as it's used in the Bible really means covenant. We call the Old and New Covenants "Old Testament" and "New Testament" because years and years ago, the people who translated the Bible from Greek into Latin used the wrong word.

In this book, we'll refer to the Old Testament as the Jewish scriptures and the New Testament as the Christian scriptures. By using the words "Jewish scriptures" we are recognizing that these writings are the sacred stories of the Jewish people, the stories of the Israelites. These sacred stories are also our sacred stories. No one so far has agreed on a good parallel term to replace "New Testament." The words "Christian scriptures" highlight the fact that the New Testament are the writings of the early communities that followed Jesus.

The **Jewish scriptures** tell the stories of the Hebrew people and God's covenant relationship with them. In this covenant God promises to be with them, strengthen them, and encourage them. God's people respond by promising to keep God's law. The **Christian scriptures** tell the stories of God's new relationship with us through Jesus Christ. His life, death, and resurrection provide a new way for us to respond to God's love freely given to us.

Christians and Jews share the books of Jewish scriptures. What we commonly call the Old Testament, Jews call the *Tanakh*. Muslims also include some of the books of the Jewish scripture and the Gospels of the Christian scripture as Holy writings.

Origins of the Bible

The Bible was written over a period of eleven hundred years — from about 1000 B.C.E. to about 100 C.E. — by many authors, editors, and communities of the ancient Near East, a region of the world we today call the Middle East, which includes the modern-day countries of Egypt, Palestine/Israel, Jordan, Syria, and Lebanon, as shown in the map on the following page. The earliest writings began as songs and stories people sang and told when they all gathered together in their homes and at religious festivals. Parents passed these stories on to their children from generation to generation and formed a shared memory of their community. These stories also helped them make choices that determined the future. The Israelites knew that they were descendants

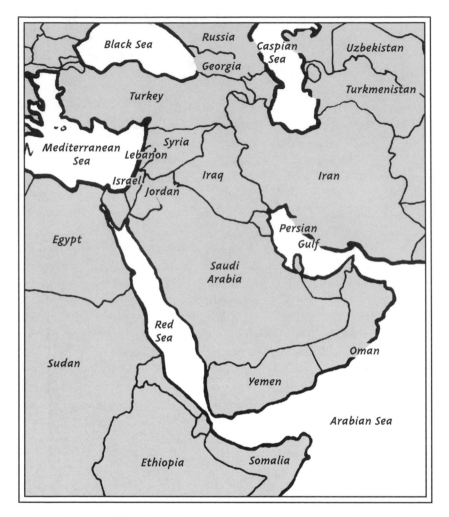

This map shows the modern-day nations of the Middle East. This is the geographic area
of the ancient Near East—the land of the people in the Bible.

of Abraham and Sarah, whom God promised would be the forebears of a great
nation. They knew that they belonged to a community that upheld the law
that Moses gave. They knew that God was on their side.

It's much like the stories we share at family gatherings, Telling and retelling
the stories of a great-grandma who served her city as mayor helps a family
remember and pass along its sense of civic duty. Knowing this history may
inspire future generations in the family to share a commitment to public
service. Every family will have a different identity and different stories.

Although some of the stories tell of people and events, the stories were not necessarily intended to relate a record of "actual events." They were meant to address basic questions of existence such as "Who are we?" and "What is the purpose of our life together?" The Israelite storytellers were sharing and celebrating the community's primary identity as the chosen people of God, and to whom God promised a specific land. The storytellers were helping their listeners remember that they were expected to live in a way that preserved their friendship with one another and with God, that is, by keeping God's law. In lots of different ways, and through many, many characters, the stories help explore this really important question: "What does it mean to say we are the people of God?"

For example, let's look at the creation stories. They are not meant to be a scientific description of how and when the world was created. They express a people's understanding of God and God's relationship to the world. God is an intimate and divine ruler of all creation and source of all blessings. God created heaven and earth. God created night and day. God created humankind in his image. And throughout the first creation story (Genesis 1:1–23), we hear the refrain, "And God saw that it was good." This is a world that is ordered by the Divine and is good.

> The book of Genesis has two creation stories. The seven-day creation story begins with Genesis 1:1 and another creation story begins with Genesis 2:4b.

Jewish Scriptures

The oldest books in the Bible are the Jewish scriptures. As the Hebrew language developed into written word, scribes began to write the stories on papyrus scrolls. The basics for the story of how the Israelites were led by Moses out of slavery in Egypt to their rise as an independent nation in Canaan, for example, is believed to have been written in the tenth century B.C.E. — a thousand years before the birth of Jesus — by a poet commissioned by King Solomon. The poet, and his scribes, did their work by hand — after all, the printing press wouldn't be invented for more than two thousand years! So, few copies would have been made. The stories were passed down from generation to generation by reciting them aloud at special meals and community worship.

More than one written tradition developed, each explaining past events in different ways, for different cultures and different circumstances. Writers of ancient sacred texts followed a rule of not deleting anything that was accepted as sacred, but they could add material. Scribes would insert contemporary ideas and practices into earlier stories, giving authority to current understandings and practices.

Ancient editors (often referred to as redactors) collected, adapted, and reinterpreted the collective stories in light of their communities' experiences. The result was not a single, clear account of a community's history and laws, but a set of stories that sometimes repeat previous accounts and sometimes even contradict one another. The intention of the editors was not to present one single perspective, but to preserve the variety of viewpoints of sacred literature. The editing likely occurred over a long period of time, but was mostly complete by the sixth century B.C.E.

By the first century C.E., Israelite communities recognized a common set of texts as the official Jewish scriptures. These texts became the **canon** or standard (the collection of books accepted as holy scripture), because they were the central texts of the Israelite community. The Jewish scripture was the Bible for the Jews at the time of Jesus and also in large part for early Christian communities. The Jewish and Christian canons of the Jewish scriptures are similar, but not identical. For example, the Roman Catholic canon (also recognized by the Episcopal Church) includes sacred Jewish writings not part of the Jewish canon. The Jewish canon has not changed since the first century C.E. and the Christian canon has not changed since the sixteenth century C.E. Finalizing the canon was a gradual process, not without controversy.

Christian Scriptures

The Christian scriptures developed differently than the Jewish scriptures. First of all, the texts of the Christian scriptures were written over a much shorter period — about a hundred years — and were written in *koine*, the common Greek that was spoken in the Roman Empire during the first century. Like the early writings of the Jewish scripture, at first news of Jesus' life, ministry, and resurrection spread by word of mouth. Early Christians believed that Jesus would return at any moment and the reign of God was about to begin, so it didn't seem necessary to write down the story of Jesus for future generations.

The earliest parts of the Christian scriptures were letters written by the apostle Paul to various Christian communities he visited, addressing the problems they faced and encouraging their new faith. These letters, written in Greek, were delivered by a messenger who read the letters aloud to the community. Paul's letters were among the earliest writings circulating among Christian communities. The earliest letter is 1 Thessalonians, believed to have been written in about 50 C.E., not quite twenty years after Jesus died.

Scholars believe that the earliest of the four Gospels, the book of Mark, was written about thirty years after Jesus' death and resurrection. Next came the Gospels of Matthew and Luke, both written sometime in the second half of the first century. It is likely that the writers of Matthew and Luke were familiar with the Gospel according to Mark, as well as a third text that no longer exists, but that scholars think probably contained sayings of Jesus.

They refer to this lost document as "Q" (*quelle*, the German word for source). Q includes sayings of Jesus common to both Matthew and Luke but not found in Mark. The last Gospel to be written was the Gospel according to John, probably completed in the last part of the first century.

All four Gospels tell the story of Jesus' life and ministry, but disagree about the details. That's because the authors had different thoughts about exactly who Jesus was, and they wrote for different audiences. Mark, for instance, ends the story with the empty tomb on Easter morning, while the other Gospels tell about the many times Jesus appeared after his resurrection.

Christian writings first circulated as codexes, folded sheets of paper stitched together and covered into notebooks. Codexes differentiated Christian from Jewish writings, which were on scrolls. Christian communities favored codexes because more could be bound together. Our familiar bound Bible didn't exist until the European-style printing press was invented in Germany in the sixteenth century.

As the stories, liturgies, hymns, and letters of the Christian community were circulated and used in worship, a common set of writings began to emerge. By the end of the fourth century, the church determined which writings were included in the canon (that is, holy scriptures). The Christian biblical canon was set. In the sixteenth century, another Roman Catholic Church council added writings — the Apocrypha — which are commonly placed between the Jewish and Christian scriptures. While the Episcopal Church recognizes these Apocrypha as scripture, most Protestant communities do not.

A VARIETY OF FORMS OF LITERATURE

As we mentioned earlier, the Bible is composed of a variety of types of literature — laws, history, fiction, hymns, romances, letters, and so on. Here's a look at some of the kinds, or genres, of literature we find in the Bible.

The Law. The **Pentateuch**, the first five books of the Bible, is a combination of laws and history. We've talked a little about history. The law, or *torah,* is the code by which people lived and determined community worship, daily living patterns, moral behavior, and business ethics. The laws with which you are likely most familiar are the Ten Commandments, the covenant law delivered by Moses. But these aren't the only laws in the Pentateuch. There are laws about how land is inherited, what to eat, and how to treat criminals. These laws were written for a particular time and don't always apply to the way we live today. Indeed, because the Pentateuch includes laws from a variety of time periods, they sometimes contradict one another.

The law of the covenant is much more than the Ten Commandments given by God to Moses. In fact, the Hebrew word for law is *torah,* which also is the word for the first five books of Jewish scripture.

Poetry. Examples of poetry in the Bible are Psalms, Proverbs, Isaiah, and Song of Songs. This poetry tells of love and life (Song of Songs), provides moral instruction (Proverbs), and provides the hymns for worship (Psalms).

Fiction. Some books are meant to be works of literary fiction. Just like today's fiction, these books aren't meant to describe actual events. Trying to determine whether the events in the book could actually have happened misses the point of fiction. A modern example is the story of George Washington cutting down the cherry tree. Whether he actually cut down the tree is not important. What is important is the truth of George Washington's character: he was an honest man. Most scholars agree that Jonah, for example, was an extended parable teaching that God is forgiving and merciful to all, not just the Israelites.

Prophecy. Many of the prophetic books (Isaiah, Hosea, and Micah, for example) include speeches given by a prophet to an audience to teach them how to live good lives. But the prophetic books also include narratives and biographies. The prophetic book Isaiah is often quoted in the Christian scriptures. Look up Mark 1:2 for an example.

Letters. We call the letters in the Christian scriptures the Epistles. The **Epistles** are letters that Paul and other apostles wrote to communities they had visited to help them address their problems and concerns. It's easy to see that these are letters by their opening words — they begin with words like "Dear So-and-So," just as we begin our letters and emails today. Paul's letters to Corinth, a town in Greece, for example, begins "To the Church of God that is in Corinth . . . Grace to you." The letters are half of a complete conversation, making them sometimes challenging to understand.

It is important to keep in mind the kind of literature you are reading in the Bible. Just as you wouldn't read a telephone book for spiritual inspiration, you wouldn't read laws in Leviticus the same way you'd read the hymns in

Psalms or the history in Exodus. The laws in Leviticus are literally legal codes that governed behavior for a particular people at a particular time, while the hymns in Psalms appeal more universally to human experiences such as joy, pain, sorrow, and forgiveness.

UNITY OF THE BIBLE

The Bible's various origins and many kinds of literature might make you wonder what keeps them together. The unity of the Bible can be understood in the **Shema,** the Hebrew declaration of faith in one God:

> *Hear, O Israel: The LORD is our God, the LORD alone.*
>
> (Deuteronomy 6:4)

This is the prayer the devout Jewish people say every day. It reminds them, as the many books of the Bible remind us all, that the Lord is our God. The Bible is the result of the interaction between human beings and the divine. The storytellers, writers, and editors were inspired to know — and to share with others — that God enters human history to care for God's people and communicate God's will. God speaks to us through the Bible.

The Bible is a witness of the Lord our God. God is the source of all life, and creation bears God's divine imprint. God is one who speaks first in creation and later leads, directs, forgives, judges, and is the end of all. Jesus is the revelation of God in the flesh, Mediator par excellence. In the Bible we find common themes of creation, sin, judgment, redemption, and restoration. The stories of the Bible narrate the events of human history toward the fulfillment of God's purpose.

With that broad introduction, let's take a closer look at the Bible.

JEWISH SCRIPTURES

The Jewish scriptures have four major divisions — the Pentateuch (Torah), the Historical Books, the Poetical and Wisdom Books, and the Prophetic Books. The thirty-nine books of the Jewish scriptures are listed in the box on the following page.

The Pentateuch (Torah)

The first five books of the Bible are known as the Pentateuch. The first eleven chapters of Genesis, the first book of the Bible, tell about the beginnings of humanity — from the creation of the world and the first people, to the fall of Adam and Eve, the Great Flood, and scattering of people into different nations

The Jewish Scriptures

Pentateuch (Torah)

Genesis	Leviticus	Deuteronomy
Exodus	Numbers	

The Historical Books

Joshua	1, 2 Samuel	Ezra
Judges	1, 2 Kings	Nehemiah
Ruth	1, 2 Chronicles	Esther

The Poetical and Wisdom Books

Job	Proverbs	Song of Solomon
Psalms	Ecclesiastes	

The Prophetic Books

Isaiah	Joel	Habakkuk
Jeremiah	Amos	Zephaniah
Lamentations	Obadiah	Haggai
Ezekiel	Jonah	Zechariah
Daniel	Micah	Malachi
Hosea	Nahum	

Note: The arrangement of these books and their divisions differ from the Jewish arrangement.

with different languages (the tower of Babel). These early stories expressed basic beliefs about the origin of the world and the nature of humans and explained why there were different kinds of people. After the story of the tower of Babel, the particular story of God's chosen people begins. It starts with the birth of Abraham, the one to whom God promised land and many descendants. Abraham was the father of the people of God.

The Jewish people call these books the Torah, the Hebrew word for law or teaching. These books contain the Law of Moses (including the Ten Commandments) and legal codes as well as the central story of God's chosen people, the nation of Israel, from the covenant established with Abraham, to the liberation of the Hebrews from Egypt, to the giving of the Ten Commandments, to the journey in the wilderness, to the death of Moses. A central theme of the Pentateuch is the covenant relationship between God and God's people. Together, the laws and the stories tell of the relationship between God and God's people, and how God's people are to live.

The Historical Books

The historical books also contain a variety of types of literature. The historical narratives in Joshua, Judges, 1 and 2 Samuel, and 1 and 2 Kings tell the continuous history of Israel from the end of Moses' life to the exile of the Israelites in Assyria and Babylon, a thousand years later in the 500s B.C.E. Dates, particularly those for stories of ancient Israel, including the flight from Egypt, are difficult to pin down.

> The historical books contain stories rich with meaning even today. The account of the widow of Zarephath in 1 Kings 17:7–24, who shows great hospitality to the prophet Elijah, for example, provides a companion for contemporary widows.

Central actions in this history are the conquest of the land by Joshua and the building of the temple by King Solomon as a place to keep the Ark of the Covenant, a chest that contained the Ten Commandments and was believed to represent God's presence among the people. During this time Israel was governed first by judges and then by kings. It faced continual threats from invaders, and at one time the kingdom divided into the Northern Kingdom (Israel) and the Southern Kingdom (Judah). Ezra and Nehemiah tell about the return of Israel from exile in Babylon. Ruth and Esther are believed to be historical fictions written to teach important lessons to the community. The historical books are rich with individual characters whose stories teach us about sin and redemption and about God's steadfast love for us.

Poetic Books and Books of Wisdom

The five books in this category contain a diversity of literature. Job, Proverbs, and Ecclesiastes are known as wisdom literature. Unlike other books in the Jewish scriptures they do not focus on the details of the nation of Israel. Instead they address individual concerns about maintaining right relationships that will lead to success and God's approval. Proverbs addresses moral life with warnings about the consequences of behavior. An example is "Do not boast about tomorrow, for you do not know what a day may bring" (Proverbs 27:1). Through the tale of the suffering of a righteous man, Job addresses the question of whether bad behavior causes human suffering, while Ecclesiastes considers suffering and joy to be a natural cycle of existence: "For everything there is a season" (Ecclesiastes 3:1).

Psalms and the Song of Solomon are books of poetry. **Psalms** are prayers sung at temple worship. Psalms express an array of human emotion — from praise to sorrow to anger. The Song of Solomon is poetry that celebrates human love.

The Prophetic Books

The prophetic books comprise mostly long speeches by prophets to a live audience, which were later written down either by the prophet or one of his associates. As with other biblical writings, later authors added biographies of the prophets, as well as editing and adding to the original statements in the book.

The age of prophets began with the rise of kings and ended during the return of the people from Babylonian exile in 538 B.C.E. Prophets, holy men and women of wisdom and vision, were called by God to play unique roles as the people's advocates to God and spokespersons for God's dream. Prophets criticized rich and powerful people and urged them to help the poor and helpless. In terms of the Lonergan imperatives, the prophets reminded the people to *be responsible*. Prophets supported social justice; prophets brought God's word to the people ("Thus says the Lord"), which often condemned current practices as against God's will. At the same time, prophets took the side of the people and begged God for mercy and forgiveness. The prophetic books bring the books of the Jewish scriptures to a close.

CHRISTIAN SCRIPTURES

The Christian scriptures are composed of twenty-seven books divided into four categories — the Gospels, history, epistles, and apocalyptic literature. These books were chosen by early church councils from among a wide range of early Christian writing based on their consistency with the teachings of the apostles, the tradition of narratives of Jesus' life and ministry, and the accepted literature of Christian communities. As we noted above, Paul's letters predate the Gospels, so, as you can see, the books do not appear in the order in which they were written.

The Christian Scriptures

Gospels

Matthew	Luke
Mark	John

History

The Acts of the Apostles

Epistles

Romans	Colossians	Hebrews
1, 2 Corinthians	1, 2 Thessalonians	James
Galatians	1, 2 Timothy	1, 2 Peter
Ephesians	Titus	1, 2, 3 John
Philippians	Philemon	Jude

Apocalyptic

The Revelation to John

The Gospels

The **Gospels** — Matthew, Mark, Luke, and John — proclaim the good news of salvation through Jesus Christ by telling about Jesus' ministry, teaching, death, and resurrection. At the time the Gospels were written, the word "gospel" referred to the announcement of a happy event such as the birth of a son or a marriage. So the Gospel according to Mark begins, "The beginning of the good news [gospel] of Jesus Christ, the son of God."

Matthew, Mark, and Luke repeat the stories and sayings of Jesus most closely. Because of their similar point of view, they are called the *synoptic* Gospels. Each, however, emphasizes different aspects of Jesus' life and teaching. Matthew presents Jesus as a great teacher and emphasizes the authority and wisdom with which Jesus interpreted Jewish law; Mark presents Jesus in terms of the great prophets of the Jewish scriptures — Elijah, Moses, and Jeremiah; Luke presents Jesus as the savior for all people and emphasizes his royal heritage as a descendant of the celebrated King David.

The traditional symbols of the four evangelists: St. Matthew as the "Divine Man"; St. Mark as a winged lion; St. Luke as the winged ox; St. John as a rising eagle.

An instructive activity is to compare the Gospels by using a *Gospel parallel*, which displays similar accounts from each Gospel next to one another. (Google "gospel parallels" to find one on the Internet.)

The Gospel according to John, the last Gospel to be written, departs markedly from the other three Gospels in terms of the chronology and details of Jesus' life. This Gospel emphasizes the divinity of Jesus (the teaching that Jesus is God) to a much greater extent than do the synoptic Gospels.

Throughout the Gospels are sayings of Jesus, parables, details of Jesus' life, and hymns sung by early Christian communities. **Parables**, stories used as metaphors for teaching, appear in the synoptic Gospels. Examples are the parables of the kingdom of God in Matthew where Jesus tells the disciples that the kingdom of God is like a treasure hidden in a field, like a mustard seed, and like yeast. Because parables teach with comparisons, or metaphors, we understand them by calling to mind our own experiences. For example, to understand the parable of the lost coins (Luke 15:8–10), we remember our own experience of losing, and then finding, something. Parables invite our thoughts and feelings, so even today they remain living instruments of instruction.

> Early Christians listened to the Gospel, sometimes for long stretches of time. Acts 20:7–11 tells the story of a young man named Eutychus, who, while listening to the apostle Paul, fell asleep and plummeted three stories out a window.

Acts of the Apostles

Acts is the account of the birth and growth of the church from the ascension of Christ to the arrival of Paul in Rome. It is a sequel to the Gospel according to Luke; scholars think it was written by the same author. Acts tells us about how the early church began, how Christianity spread, and how early Christian communities addressed its problems. A central figure in Acts is the apostle Paul, a Jew who grew up in the Greek city of Tarsus.

Paul experienced a dramatic vision of Christ, converted to Christianity, and dedicated his life to establishing and guiding Christian communities. Two central themes of Acts are that the church continues the history of the Jewish people and that gentiles, or non-Jews, are welcome into Christian communities and can share God's promise of salvation. By portraying the expansion of the early church as being led by the Holy Spirit, Acts provides early Christians the confidence that their communities are living according to God's will.

The Epistles

The Epistles are a set of twenty-one letters and writings in the form of letters. Thirteen were written either by the apostle Paul or by one of his followers in Paul's name. Paul's letters (except Romans) were sent to early Christian communities he had established during his mission journeys throughout the eastern part of the Mediterranean to provide them with continued guidance. The map shows these communities.

This map of the Mediterranean shows major communities that Paul visited.

Letters were a common way for leaders of various church communities to communicate. They address issues such as leadership and gift for ministry, as well as questions such as when the Messiah — Jesus, the savior promised by God — would return and whether Gentiles had to follow Jewish law to join a Christian community.

Deuterocanonical Writings

Tobit	Sirach (Ecclesiasticus)
Judith	Baruch
Esther (additions)	1–4 Maccabees
Wisdom of Solomon	Daniel (additions)

Reading the Epistles can be like listening to one end of a telephone conversation. We know one side of the conversation from the letters that we have in the Bible, but we don't have the letters that asked the questions or posed the problems in the first place. We sometimes have to guess what the initial problem or question was as well as the details of the particular issue.

The Revelation to John

The Revelation to John is a vision that is meant to sustain early Christians in the face of persecution. Revelation was written during a time when the world was hostile to Christians and when acknowledging yourself to be a Christian could lead to death. With great symbolism and complexity the author assures a church under persecution that Christ is with them, encouraging them to keep faith. Revelation can be a difficult book to understand without a good commentary or teacher to guide the reader, who needs to be especially careful not to interpret it simplistically or take its confusing symbolism literally.

The Apocrypha

The thirty-nine books of the Jewish scriptures and twenty-seven books of the Christian scriptures make up the sixty-six books of the Bible. In addition to these books, the Episcopal Church (along with the Roman Catholic Church) also recognizes the deuterocanonical texts listed in the box as holy scripture.

These additional books are known as **Apocrypha**, meaning "things hidden away," or deuterocanonical, meaning "second canon" because they were added to the Christian canon in the sixteenth century, about twelve hundred years after the first Christian canon was established. These additional books, generally located between the Jewish and Christian scriptures, are literature found in either the ancient Greek translation of the Jewish scriptures, called the Septuagint, or in Latin translations of the Greek, but are not contained in the Jewish scriptures. In the sixteenth century, the Roman Catholic Church accepted them into the canon, and the Church of England followed suit. Most Protestant churches do not recognize deuterocanonical literature as holy scripture. The Apocrypha include histories, historical fiction, wisdom, devotional writings, letters, and an apocalypse (a vision of the end times).

READING THE BIBLE

Why Read the Bible?

We read the Bible for a variety of reasons. The Bible reveals God's walk with God's people and with us. The Bible reveals who God is and who we are as creatures of God. Through the Bible we learn about God's promises to us and about how to live within the covenant relationship. We may be able to recite the commandment that Jesus gave: "Love one another as I have loved you" (John 15:12). The Bible guides us in how to apply this commandment, as well as the two greatest commandments: "You shall love the Lord your God with all your heart and with all your soul, and with all your mind." And "You shall love your neighbor as yourself" (Matthew 22:37–39).

The Bible is neither self-help, nor a rulebook, nor God's answers to moral questions, and certainly not a weapon with which to put others down.

It won't tell you for whom to vote in an election, but it can guide your important decisions. Through the Bible, we come to know the very presence of God — a God who cares, guides, strengthens, comforts, and inspires us through the stories, hymns, and sayings of God's people. We are transformed by the knowledge that we are beloved creations and we seek to live in ways that reflect that knowledge.

Read the Bible in Community

So Philip ran up to it [the chariot of an Ethiopian eunuch] and heard him reading the prophet Isaiah. He asked, "Do you understand what you are reading?" He replied, "How can I, unless someone guides me?" And he invited Philip to get in and sit beside him. (Acts 8:30–31)

This conversation between Philip and a eunuch in Acts reminds us that we are meant to read the Bible with others. The Bible is a public book, a book about community to be heard, studied, and engaged in the company of others.

The Episcopal Church firmly recognizes the Bible as a public book. Each Sunday we usually read four passages from the Bible — a reading from the

Jewish scriptures, a psalm, a reading from the Epistles, and a Gospel reading. The readings are selected according to the **lectionary**, a three-year cycle (denoted as Years A, B, and C) of passages of the Bible read at church services. Over a three-year period, you will hear almost all of the Christian scriptures and a good chunk of the Jewish scriptures. We also hear scriptures in our hymns and prayers found in the Book of Common Prayer. Hymn 645 ("The King of love my shepherd is"), for example, is based on Psalm 23. Our service of Holy Communion is filled with scriptural references. The Sanctus ("Holy, holy, holy") is based on Isaiah 6:3 and Revelation 4:8. The words of institution during the prayers of the Eucharist are based on 1 Corinthians 11:23–25. (A familiar joke among Episcopalians is that upon reading the Bible they are amazed at how often it quotes the Book of Common Prayer.) Through worship, we turn the hymns, letters, and stories of the Bible into prayer.

Hearing the Bible in community gives us the opportunity to see the variety of interpretations through the sermon, in the hymns, and in conversations about the sermon. By reading the Bible in community we can share our insights and understandings with one another. The wisdom and insights of the community widen our biblical understanding, add richness of interpretation, and encourage us to think carefully about the biblical words we hear.

Hearing the Bible in worship also provides a particular context for the Bible. That is, we hear the stories of the Bible in light of the good news that God loves us so much that God came to live among us as Jesus Christ. And through Christ, God gives us enduring love and forgiveness.

When reading anywhere in the Bible, be attentive: What is the author saying? What version am I reading? New Revised Standard Version? New International Version? King James? How might the words differ in another version? Be intelligent. What have I understood? Are there other ways to understand this? Be reasonable: Among several understandings, which is best? Is there a best understanding? How might my understanding change if I discussed it in community? Be responsible: Based on how I understand what I've read, is there something of value I ought to do?

Here are five steps to read a passage in the Bible:

1. *Read the passage and ask what's important. Circle key words and phrases. Share these phrases with others in your study group.*

Of course, the first step is to choose a reading. One discipline is to look at the readings for the coming Sunday or in the Daily Office listed in your Book of Common Prayer. These readings begin and end in logical places, such as the beginning and ending of a story or parable, and provide a set of readings that will help you become familiar with the diversity of experiences of God.

Steps for Reading the Bible

Don't get frustrated if you find that reading the Bible isn't easy. It isn't! But there are some things you can do to guide your reading. Chapter 8 discusses one method, called *lectio divina,* in which the readers focus on just a few words or phrases in a Bible passage and ask God to guide them to understand what those words and phrases are saying to them. Here are steps to read the Bible with both your mind and heart:

1. Read the passage and ask what's important. Circle key words and phrases. Share these phrases with others in your study group.

2. Read the passage again, writing down any questions that come to mind. Share your questions and look together for answers.

3. Read the verses immediately before and after the passage.

4. Discuss the main themes of the passage.

5. Ask what the passage is calling you to do, and share your reflections.

The downside of choosing readings this way is that some parts of the Bible are not in the lectionary cycle and you may want to read longer selections than those in the lectionary.

Read the passage. Is there anything that catches your attention? Circle key words and phrases. Reading and hearing the Bible today is how the Bible remains the living word of God. While the text itself does not change, the readers do. It is likely that others in your group will be drawn to different words and phrases. We hear the stories of the Bible through our own experiences. With the guidance of the Holy Spirit these stories become our stories.

2. *Read the passage again, writing down any questions that come to mind. Share your questions and look together for answers.*

While you read the passage the second time, write down your questions. General questions might be about how to approach the passage. Is it a hymn, a historical writing, or a code of law? Does the passage refer to unfamiliar cultural beliefs and practices? Do you recognize the characters and events in the passage?

Help one another find the answers. One place to look is in introductory essays and notes found in annotated Bibles as well as in other books that comment on the Bible. Introductory essays will answer general questions such as these:

- ◆ What is the type of literature?

- ◆ Who wrote it?

- ◆ When was it likely written?

- ◆ What are the main themes?

A commentary might discuss customs and ways of thinking of the time and symbolism as well as additional word translations. Remember, the Bible wasn't first written in English. It had to be translated, and there are many translations available. You may even want to ask members of your group to read from different English translations for comparison.

Context is crucial to understanding. It will help you understand, for example, that the prescription in Exodus "an eye for an eye, a tooth for a tooth" (Exodus 21:23–25) is a law that *limited* retribution at a time when vengeance allowed was unlimited. As you continue your study of the Bible, you will improve your skills for answering questions and grow in your knowledge of the world in which the Bible was written. Don't worry if you cannot find answers to all your questions. But continue to keep them in mind as you explore the meaning of the passage.

3. *Read the verses immediately before and after the passage.*

The verses just before and after the passage often provide great insight into the meaning of your reading. For example, the story of the woman who poured very expensive oil over Jesus' head in Matthew 26 comes just before the Last Supper. Knowing this context shows us that her action wasn't a random act of adoration; pouring oil on Jesus was preparing his body for death and, for readers, foreshadows the crucifixion.

4. *Discuss the main themes of the passage.*

Once you have a sense of the context, look back at the words and phrases you circled. These will help you identify the main themes of the passage. Discuss these themes with people in your group. Ask each other if these themes remind you of other stories in the Bible. If so, which ones? See if these themes remind you of experiences in your own life. Do these other stories help you understand the passage? If you were reading the eye-for-an-eye passage in Exodus, you might remember that Jesus taught a new standard of mercy and forgiveness: to love your enemies, to do good to those who hate you, and to turn the other cheek (Luke 6:29 and Matthew 5:39).

5. *Ask what the passage is calling you to do, and share your reflections.*

The final step is to apply the themes and messages to your thoughts and faith today. The Bible is the living word of God meant to help us understand God, ourselves, and our world. Ask one another, "How does this passage challenge your thoughts and beliefs?" Again, be aware of the original context of the writing. The Bible was written by people living in a specific time and culture that was probably quite different from yours. Consider your answer in terms of the practices and teaching of your faith community. Your faith community can be particularly helpful with this final step. A community will give you a variety of viewpoints, provide wisdom of knowledge and experience, and help you explore the meaning of the passage in your life.

READ THE BIBLE: IT'S OUR WALK WITH GOD

The Bible reflects our central beliefs: The Lord is our God, the Lord alone; God freed us from our life of sin by sending his only Son, Jesus. Read the Bible as a story that tells you who God is, who you are, and what we are called to do as people of God. The struggles of the people you read about in the Bible are often a lot like our struggles today. The life, ministry, and teachings of Jesus will help guide us in our lives today. His death and resurrection gives us new life today.

✝ TRANSFORMING QUESTIONS

1. **Be Attentive:** Find the readings for the coming Sunday, choose one, and read it slowly. (The website *textweek.com* provides the Revised Common Lectionary readings.) What happens in the reading? Who are the characters? What do they say and do? Does anything surprise you?

2. **Be Intelligent:** What situation today does the reading address? What is the reading saying?

3. **Be Reasonable:** Consult a commentary. (The *HarperCollins Bible Commentary* is an example.) What do others say about the meaning of the reading? Do these sources bring new insight?

4. **Be Responsible:** What is the reading calling you to do?

5. **Be in Love Transformed:** What does this exercise suggest about how you might approach reading the Bible?

Chapter Four

History

FOUR WORDS TOWARD AHA:
TODAY WE REMEMBER TOMORROW

Four words stopped me in place. I now pray them when I prepare to celebrate Eucharist. A colleague at Diocesan House, about to preside at our weekly Eucharist, explained that we would use the readings and prayers assigned for the next day. She concluded: "Today we remember tomorrow."

The words sang. *Today* (any day), *we* (three or three hundred) *remember* (we give thanks by remembering) *tomorrow*. Imagine remembering tomorrow! Remembering God's promises, we project our hope.

As we make Eucharist, we pray: "We give thanks...for the goodness and love you have made known to us in creation, in the calling of Israel to be your people, in your Word spoken though the prophets, and above all in the Word made flesh, Jesus your Son....On the night before he died for us, he took bread....Do this for the remembrance of me. After supper, he took the cup of wine...he gave it to them....Drink this...for the remembrance of me." Give thanks. Remember. Hope.

A former nun is the protagonist of the novel *Severina* by Italian author Ignazio Silone. As she lay dying, a sister from her former convent takes her hand: "Severina, tell me you believe." Severina says, "No...*but I hope.*"

Might you express your faith that way? You've wondered about God, about how God is represented, about history. You hope, you trust, you remember...tomorrow.

"There is but one fundamental truth for Christians." Bethlehem bishop Paul Marshall preached on All Souls' Day. "In Christ we are tied to God and each other in a way that the circumstances of time and space cannot defeat. One day we will be the ones remembered, held in the minds and hearts of those slightly behind us in the grand procession toward the heart of God." Doing what we do today in the words and hymns of this liturgy, we "gently heal our past and calmly embrace our future."

That you are reading this book suggests that you have had some history with God. You may be seeking to discover the radical center of your faith and hope: acknowledging that Jesus Christ is Lord. Do not allow anyone or anything to domesticate that radical center.

God challenges us to dream. To pray is to dream, to hope, to expect, to trust, to imagine. Whether worshiping with a community, reading alone, reflecting on the Bible, considering a personal experience, a story, or a movie, we are at work in an ecosystem of prayer, the research and development aspect of the church.

Only the pray-er knows that the really real is God breaking into human history — breaking through our prejudices and preferred notions with questions about poor and powerless persons, about justice and peace, about personal and systemic transformation so we might break out with new God-given hearts to pursue God's heart's desires.

Looking deeply within their souls, saints find God. Allow God to transform you and the world around you. Don't let anyone de-fine and re-duce reality for you. Don't let anyone imprison you in that most secure prison without walls, without the context of history, the prison you don't know you're in, the prison of *non-saints*. Imagine the reality of God. See things differently. Remember tomorrow.

Look back on your history. Have you not been drawn by God? Look back on the idols you have abandoned. Might you be at a stage in your life where you are coming to believe less, but more so?

The 1990 film *Avalon* begins in the pretelevision living room of an immigrant family. Children sitting around a family elder listen intently to the storyteller, who always begins with "I came to America in 1914."

A few years later, where family, church, and synagogue once told the stories children grew into, television became the new storyteller. With one reason for being: to deliver an audience to an advertiser. The new storyteller neither knew nor loved the children.

As a servant of our market economy, television suggested that I am what I buy, that happiness has to do with material acquisition, that consumption is inherently good, and that property, wealth, and power are more important than people. "But it cannot be like that with you," Jesus says.

The new storyteller has given us the two most dangerous words of the [twentieth] century, according to the late Neil Postman: "*Now . . . this* — to ease the transition from a report on a natural disaster to a commercial about your desperate need for an electric toothbrush." With these words, Postman contends, the new storyteller promotes a dangerous discontinuity.

Toward the end of *Avalon,* the old storyteller, taken at his request to his old Baltimore neighborhood, saw that it had so completely changed that he no longer knew it. "If I knew things would no longer be," he said, "I would have tried to have remembered better."

Today, we remember tomorrow.   *— B.L.*

◆   ◆   ◆

As Bill reminds us, we already have a history with God. And your history is part of a long history. Just as you have been drawn by God, countless saints before have also been drawn and have marched toward the heart of God. So let us hear their witness so that we can continue on our march and remember tomorrow.

THE BIRTH OF THE CHURCH

So those who welcomed his message were baptized, and that day about three thousand persons were added. They devoted themselves to the apostle's teaching and fellowship, to the breaking of bread and the prayers.

(Acts 2:41–42)

Fifty days after the resurrection of Jesus, on the day of **Pentecost**, the Holy Spirit descended from heaven like a violent wind. The apostles began to speak in other languages. Filled with the Holy Spirit, they began to live into the **Great Commission** that Jesus had given them:

Go therefore and make disciples of all nations, baptizing them in the name of the Father and of the Son and of the Holy Spirit, and teaching them to obey everything that I have commanded you. And remember, I am with you always, to the end of the age. (Matthew 28:19–20)

As the people of God — the church — we are called to this same great commission, which, as we sing in Hymn 527, is to "heal the sick and preach the word." How do you understand the great commission?

On that day of Pentecost the apostles baptized those who believed, about three thousand. We celebrate this day each year as Pentecost, the birthday of the church. The Greek word translated as "church" is *ekklesia,* which literally means those gathered, or the congregation. The word "church" in this sense does not refer to a building, but to a community of believers.

After Jesus' resurrection, the apostles spread the teachings of Jesus first in Jewish communities near Jerusalem and later during mission journeys outside Jerusalem. These early communities understood themselves to be Jews who followed Jesus, a reform movement within Judaism. It was not until about 90 C.E., nearly sixty years after Jesus' death and resurrection, that the followers of Christ began to be called "Christians."

The apostle Paul played an important part in spreading Christianity. We read in Acts 9 that Paul started out zealously persecuting followers of Jesus, but on the road to Damascus, a few years after Jesus died, everything changed. Paul met Jesus for the first time through a vision telling him to spread the good news to the gentiles (people who were not descendants of the Israelites). Paul and his partners began to establish Christian communities throughout the area around the Mediterranean Sea, which was at that time controlled by the Romans and was part of the Roman Empire. These early Christian communities, who believed the world as they knew it would end soon when Jesus returned, shared meals, teachings, and prayers in one another's homes. New converts joined the community through baptism, and they broke bread to remember Christ's death and resurrection. Baptism and the breaking of the bread are the two central sacraments of the church today.

The apostle Paul became a follower of Jesus after a conversion experience that led him to change. Throughout his letters, he developed a theology and a morality that might be summed up in this way: "Because Christ lives within you, you are something new. You are a new creation. That's the theology. And this is the morality: Therefore, *be* who you are. *Live* as a new creature." Be attentive in your own life to experiences that might lead you to change in some way.

Communities of the Early Church

The map on page 43 shows the location of many early church communities. Antioch, Ephesus, Alexandria, Corinth, and Rome, the larger cities of the Roman Empire connected by trading routes, had big Christian communities. During the first few hundred years after Jesus' resurrection, the rest of the world had no — or at least very little — knowledge of Jesus. Christianity began as small communities in a specific region of the world — the Roman Empire — and from there it spread from Asia into Europe and Africa. During the fifteenth century, European colonization spread Christianity to the Americas. Today Christian churches exist throughout the world.

Episkopos *in the Early Church*

The apostles were the leaders of the early church and had the authority of Jesus' teaching. The leader of a local Christian community was called *episkopos,* or "overseer." The word "Episcopal" in fact comes from the Greek word *episkopos*, and the English word for *episkopos* is "bishop." In the Episcopal Church, the bishop oversees the diocese, the primary unit of the Episcopal Church. Early church leaders were also referred to as *presbyteros* (presbyter, or priest) and *diakonos* (deacon). Today the Episcopal Church has a three-fold ordained ministry of bishop, priest, and deacon, each with a distinct role in the church. The apostles passed their authority to local leaders by laying their hands on new leaders. The continuation of the authority of the apostles' teaching by the laying on of hands is called **apostolic succession**. Apostolic succession and a threefold ministry of bishops, priests, and deacons are defining characteristics of the Episcopal Church.

THE ROMAN EMPIRE TO THE MIDDLE AGES

In 324 C.E., Constantine became the first Roman emperor to legalize Christianity. Until that time, Christians were periodically persecuted by fines, imprisonment, and even death for refusing to worship Roman gods. When Constantine gained control over the entire Roman Empire, he moved its capital from Rome to Byzantium, in what is now the city of Istanbul, Turkey. He renamed the city "Nova Roma," or New Rome, but it was popularly known as Constantinople (the city of Constantine). Constantinople later became the center of Eastern Orthodox Christianity, while Rome became the center of Western Catholic Christianity. Constantine saw Christianity as a way to unify his vast empire and began the process of creating a uniform belief by calling the bishops together in 325 C.E. to Nicea, located in the present-day city of Iznik, Turkey. Their job was to find a common understanding of who Jesus was and his place in history. The result was the Nicene Creed, which we recite at church every Sunday.

By the fifth century, the Roman Empire had grown weak from invasion by tribes from northern Europe and political fighting in Rome. The end of Roman rule began the eleven-hundred-year period from about 400 to 1500 C.E. that we call the **Middle Ages**. The Western empire (Europe) broke into small regions with numerous languages, each ruled by different kings and noblemen. The church provided both religious and cultural unity for Europe. The Roman emperor ruled the eastern part of the Roman Empire until 1453, when the Muslim Turkish rulers from Asia conquered the city of Byzantium.

During the Middle Ages, communities were organized around land owned by local noblemen and protected by knights. The peasants worked the land and produced goods for the nobility in exchange for protection. The church, particularly monasteries, owned much of the land and became increasingly involved in social, political, and business aspects of daily life. Many monasteries were responsible for the spiritual as well as the economic and physical well-being of the people. Monks and nuns prepared medicine, sewed, and taught reading and writing. Monasteries were also the libraries for society and preserved important early Christian writings. We see how important the church was to life in the Middle Ages by the magnificent cathedrals in city and town centers such as the cathedral of Notre Dame in Chartres, France.

"The experiment of St. Benedict, St. Francis [both monks]...represented the revolt of a heroic soul against surrounding apathy and decadence; an invasion of novelty; a sharp break with society" (Evelyn Underhill).[4] What response does the witness of St. Benedict call from us?

The Middle Ages were also the time of the Crusades. You may have seen movies such as *Kingdom of Heaven* or learned about the Crusades in your courses. The Crusades, which lasted about a hundred years, were launched in 1095 by the church to recover the Holy Land — the region of the world where stories of the Bible took place and where Jesus lived — from the Muslims. The kings and other leaders in Europe supported the Crusades to acquire land, riches, and control over trading routes. During the Crusades all non-Christians, especially Jews and Muslims, were targets of persecution.

THE REFORMATION

As the Roman Catholic Church grew more wealthy and powerful, church leaders limited the people's freedom to express opposing ideas. The church used its power over the spiritual lives of the people to sell indulgences — pieces of paper that guaranteed entry into heaven. Some people believed indulgences were abuses of church power and violated the teachings of the Bible.

People began to protest these and other practices and called for reforms. This movement, which gained momentum in the sixteenth century, is called the **Reformation. Martin Luther** of Germany and **John Calvin** of France were two leaders of the Reformation in Europe.

Martin Luther's most famous act was nailing ninety-five theses — or arguments — on the door of the castle church in Wittenberg in 1517. The theses stated his disputes with the Roman Catholic Church, including the selling of indulgences. He argued against Roman Catholic Church teaching that salvation came through the church. Instead, Luther promoted a doctrine called **justification by grace through faith**, which states that God gives

---

4. Evelyn Underhill, *The Life of the Spirit and the Life of To-day* (New York: E. P Dutton, 1922), 6.

people salvation freely. We do not earn salvation through good deeds, but we can accept it with faith. Luther believed that people didn't need the church between them and God and that sacraments weren't necessary for salvation. God's grace was sufficient.

Meanwhile in France, John Calvin accepted Luther's doctrine of justification by grace through faith. But he also believed in the fundamental doctrine of predestination. Predestination is the belief that God directs the course of history down to the smallest detail. It is the job of people to maintain the order created by God. The Reformation resulted in the establishment of Protestant churches that broke with the traditional practices of the Roman Catholic Church. Both Luther and Calvin were important to this movement.

In earlier centuries, some people had opposed church doctrine. So what made the Protestant Reformation take off in the sixteenth century? Historians agree that the printing press played a big part in the Reformation's success. The printing press, first used in Europe in the mid-1400s, allowed dissenting opinions to be widely distributed, strengthening the Reformation movement.

The Reformation and the printing press also helped make it possible to produce early translations of the Bible from Latin, the official language of the church, to languages that people spoke every day, such as French, German, or English. New doctrines encouraged people to come to their own decisions about belief, so they needed to read the Bible in their own languages. By 1524, Luther had translated the Christian scriptures to German, and by 1526 **William Tyndale** had translated them into English. This brought the words of the Bible and its interpretation into the hands of all believers, not just educated clergy and monks.

England during the Reformation

The Episcopal Church traces its roots directly to the Church of England, which, until **Henry VIII,** was part of the Roman Catholic Church. The Church of England had always recognized the pope in Rome as the head of the church, and at first King Henry supported the pope during the Reformation. For his loyal support, the pope named Henry "Defender of the Faith." Soon after, though, a dispute erupted. Henry asked the pope to annul, or end, his marriage with Catherine of Aragon because she did not bear him a son to inherit the throne. The pope refused. So in 1534 King Henry issued an "Act of Supremacy," which made him head of the Church of England, splitting the Church of England from the Roman Catholic Church.

To make worship understandable to the common person, **Thomas Cranmer**, archbishop of Canterbury, compiled the Book of Common Prayer. Published in 1549 during the reign of King Edward VI, this prayer book is the first to present daily and Sunday services in English and in one volume. It is the book from which our 1979 Book of Common Prayer comes.

Queen Elizabeth, 1533–1603.

In 1553 Queen Mary I restored England to Roman Catholicism, but in 1558 Queen Elizabeth I inherited the throne and within one year reestablished an independent Church of England. The Act of Uniformity (1559) made the Book of Common Prayer the official book of prayer for the Church of England. With Queen Elizabeth, the Anglican Church was set on a path to being a people of common prayer, rather than common belief.

Because the Church of England did not split over theological reasons, unlike the Protestant churches, the Church of England maintained many of the practices and beliefs of the Roman Catholic Church, including its system of government by bishops and its style of worship. Like Protestant churches, the Church of England worshiped in the language of the people, in this case English, and the Church of England affirmed that salvation comes from God's grace, not the deeds of the believer.

I have no desire to make windows into men's souls.
—quote attributed to Queen Elizabeth I

THE CHURCH OF ENGLAND IN NORTH AMERICA

The Episcopal Church is uniquely American. Our history has greatly affected who we are, how we worship together, and how we govern ourselves. And it will continue to help define us into the future.

Just as Americans began to see themselves as a new nation apart from England and the crown, members of the Church of England in America also saw their church as separate from the Church of England. In 1607 the settlement town of Jamestown, Virginia, organized itself as a parish with a priest brought from England and supported its clergy with local government taxes. Because these settlers provided for their own financial needs, they began to see themselves as independent of the Church of England. The situation was a little different in the northern colonies because taxes in northern New England supported the Congregational Church, not the Church of England. In New England, members of the Church of England retained greater ties to England because religious societies in England paid for their priests. During the colonial period, no bishops ever visited America. The leaders of the Church of England and the British Parliament did not want to grant American communities the independence that having a bishop would provide. But the colonists didn't really mind — as long as they had a sufficient number of priests, they were happy to be far from the rule of the Church of England.

American Bishops

After the Revolution the New England Anglicans wanted to organize themselves formally and felt they needed a bishop. In June 1783 they sent **Samuel Seabury**, the rector at a church in the state of New York, to England to be ordained a bishop. Because Samuel Seabury was an American citizen, and couldn't take the oath of the King's Supremacy, the English bishops couldn't ordain him a bishop. Seabury turned to the bishops in Scotland, who were not bound by English law. In November 1784, they ordained Samuel Seabury as the first American bishop.

Two years later, Parliament granted the archbishop of Canterbury the right to ordain three bishops who would not be asked to swear an allegiance to the crown. By 1790 three American bishops had been ordained as bishops, a sufficient number to bring the historic episcopate, or system of governance by bishops, to America.

The Birth of the Episcopal Church

When Samuel Seabury returned to America, he began to unify various Anglican churches as one American Episcopal Church. It wasn't an easy job. The communities in the North wanted to have bishops while those in the South had become accustomed to governing themselves without a bishop. The two groups compromised: They would have bishops, but the priests and members of the congregation would help choose bishops and write church canons, or laws.

In 1789, the leaders of the new Episcopal Church wrote a constitution. It said that bishops would be elected by priests and members of the congregation instead of being appointed by the king or queen as was done in England. The Episcopal Church would be governed by two houses — the House of Bishops, comprised only of bishops, and the House of Deputies, comprised of priests and general church members. Laws can originate in either house, but both houses must agree on them. The two-house system was much like the two-house system of the U.S. Congress.

The year 1789 was a banner year for the Episcopal Church. It held its first General Convention, passed its constitution, and adopted the first American **Book of Common Prayer**. The American Book of Common Prayer was much the same as the prayer book in England, minus prayers for the king and royal family. Plus, it added a call to the Holy Spirit, or **epiclesis**, to the Eucharistic prayer, a modification Samuel Seabury had promised to the Scottish bishops when he was ordained bishop.

Samuel Seabury was the
Episcopal Church's first American bishop.

THE EPISCOPAL CHURCH IN THE 1800s

The Episcopal Church continued to be shaped by the life and culture of the United States. During the 1800s the West was settled, the Civil War was fought, American industry expanded, and a great number of people from Ireland, Germany, Scandinavia, southern Europe, and Asia immigrated to the United States. Immigration changed the country from a nation of people with largely British background to a diverse people with a variety of practices and beliefs. Worship practices and social activity became likewise more diverse in the Episcopal Church.

Westward Expansion and Missionaries

During the first few decades, the Episcopal Church struggled. General Conventions were poorly attended, several dioceses had no bishops, and membership did not grow. But along came **John Henry Hobart,** with his great energy and enthusiasm for evangelism. As bishop of New York from 1816 to 1830, he was responsible for establishing Episcopal churches in nearly every major town in New York state, increasing their number from 50 to 170. During his first four years as bishop, the number of priests and deacons doubled and the number of missionaries quadrupled. By 1820 the number of Episcopal churches in the United States had doubled to four hundred.

In 1835, the General Convention ordained missionary bishops who, instead of overseeing an established diocese, were sent to the frontier to establish new dioceses. **Jackson Kemper** was the first missionary bishop. Traveling by horseback and open wagon he organized eight dioceses and established two colleges. Kemper worked particularly among Potawatomi, Seneca, Oneida, and Huron Indians, urged the church to pay more attention to Native Americans, and encouraged the translation of the Bible and the prayer book into their native languages.

Jackson Kemper ordained **Enmegahbowh,** an Odawa (Ottawa) Indian from Canada, as a deacon in 1859. Twelve years later in 1867, Enmegahbowh became the first recognized Native American priest in the Episcopal Church. In 1869, Paul Mazakute was ordained the first Dakota priest, and in 1881, **David Pendleton Oakerhater** became the first Cheyenne deacon. These men worked hard, often without the support of the national church, to spread the gospel among Native America people.

The church's hard work in the missions paid off. From 1820 to 1859, the number of Episcopal congregations grew more than fivefold from 400 to 2,120.

African Americans and the Civil War

America was a place of slavery and racial bigotry. Just after the Revolutionary War, eight hundred thousand African Americans were slaves; only fifty-nine thousand lived as free citizens. America was also a place of great change. **Absalom Jones**, who was born in 1746 into slavery, purchased his wife's and his own freedom and later became the first African American to be ordained a priest in the Episcopal Church. Jones and other blacks had left St. George's Methodist Church in Philadelphia when its vestry decided that all African Americans had to sit in the balcony, apart from the whites. He and others walked out and began another

Absalom Jones was the first African American Episcopal priest. He was ordained in 1802.

church that later joined the Episcopal Church, as St. Thomas African Episcopal Church. Before the Civil War began, fifteen other African Americans were ordained Episcopal priests.

Just as the nation was divided about slavery across North–South lines, so was the Episcopal Church. Southern agriculture depended on slave labor. Southern Episcopal plantation owners built churches for their black slaves, who were ministered to by white clergy. Northerners, for the most part, supported abolition, but some northern white churches segregated their members according to the color of their skin. The Episcopal Church never took an official position on slavery.

When the South seceded from the United States and declared itself a separate nation, many southern dioceses organized themselves as a breakaway church called the Protestant Episcopal Church in the Confederate States of America. The northern church did not recognize the split and continued to list southern bishops on the roster at general conventions. At the end of the Civil War, the southern dioceses were invited to return to the Episcopal Church; in 1865, the Episcopal Church was once again united.

Rise of Industry and the Church's Response to Social Problems

After the end of the Civil War, American industry grew by leaps and bounds, moving from fourth to first largest in the entire world. As people moved away from farms and small towns to seek jobs — and opportunity — in the factories, newcomers came to America from other countries, and our cities grew quickly. But the factories offered poor working conditions, low wages, and long hours. Many employed children. Two new social classes emerged — the working poor and the wealthy capitalists (those with money to build the factories and earn profits). New social problems appeared: unemployment, unsafe working conditions, child labor, and poor housing.

Episcopalians, who believe strongly in helping people in need, responded with action. Trinity Church Wall Street in New York City, a wealthy parish that owned a lot of land there, fixed up the apartments they owned to help improve housing conditions for the working poor. The Women's Auxiliary, organized in 1871, provided most of the funding for churchwide programs to help the poor. In 1883, **William Rainsford**, rector at St. George's in New York City, created clubs for girls, boys, women, and men, as well as societies for different interest groups. He also built church schools with gyms for the city's poor children and started parish nursing programs.

Earlier in the 1800s, many churches were unfriendly places for people who were poor and uneducated. It was not uncommon for churches to raise funds by charging rent to sit in a pew on Sunday morning. **William Augustus Muhlenberg**, founder of the Church of the Holy Communion in New York City, eliminated the pew tax. He also started a parish school, a parish unemployment fund, and a fresh-air fund to send poor city children to the country for the summer. Muhlenberg also introduced his church to some traditionally Roman Catholic practices, such as weekly communion, altar flowers, choir robes, Christmas greens, and special services for Holy Week, the days when Christians recall Jesus' crucifixion and death. But Muhlenberg still retained the Protestant emphasis on a personal relationship with God.

So let the name brotherhood prevail, let there be no differences of worldly rank, in the Church of the Holy Communion.   —William Augustus Muhlenberg[5]

The Oxford Movement

Muhlenberg's introduction of "Roman Catholic" traditions paved the way for other "high-church" practices in other parishes around the country. Followers of the **Oxford Movement,** started in England in 1833, wanted the Episcopal Church to readopt Roman Catholic practices such as putting candles on the altar, having priests wear chasubles and other vestments, processing with a cross, and bowing at the passing of the cross. With huge numbers of immigrants from Roman Catholic backgrounds arriving in America during these years, many newcomers to the Episcopal Church felt at home with these rituals.

Many other people, however, were offended by these rituals and felt they were too similar to Roman Catholic practices. They worried that these formal rituals would make the Episcopal Church similar to the Roman Catholic Church in other ways, too. They feared that a more "Roman" Episcopal church would try to exert power over people's individual beliefs.

This controversy, known as the "ritualist controversy," was a big deal. For example, the bishop of the Diocese of Massachusetts refused to visit a Boston church because it had candles and a crucifix on the altar and its rector wore vestments. In 1868 the General Convention considered a proposal to ban such practices. But presiding bishop John Henry Hopkins felt that diversity was good for the church and kept most of these practices in place. Only bowing and lifting the bread and the wine during Eucharist as acts of adoration were forbidden.

---

5. *The Gospel Messenger and Church Record of Western New York,* Utica, August 3, 1844.

THE EPISCOPAL CHURCH IN THE 1900s and EARLY 2000s

The 1900s were marked by concerns for worldwide church unity, continuing social issues, and the role of women in the church.

Church Unity

In the late 1800s and early 1900s, American church leaders wondered whether the various American church denominations (Baptist, Methodist, Lutheran, Roman Catholic) could address modern problems more effectively as one body. William Reed Huntington, an Episcopal priest, outlined four

principles that the Episcopal Church believes are necessary to restore all denominations as one church. This important document for the Episcopal Church became known as the Chicago Quadrilateral and appears on pages 876–77 of the Book of Common Prayer in the section called "Historical Documents." In the early 1900s, **Charles Henry Brent,** an Episcopal bishop, led the way toward worldwide ecumenical discussions. In 1927, he presided over the World Conference on Faith and Order,

The World Council of Churches website is *oikoumene.org.*

which later became part of the **World Council of Churches,** a fellowship of more than 340 Christian denominations worldwide.

The Episcopal Church continues to work toward unity with other churches. In 1950 the Episcopal Church helped found the National Council of Churches (*www.ncccusa.org*). In 2000 the Episcopal Church and the Evangelical Lutheran Church of America established full communion with one another. The two churches fully recognize each other's members, ministries, and sacraments and can share one another's priests and pastors. Formal discussions of communion continue between the Episcopal Church and the Moravian and Presbyterian Churches.

Twenty-seven percent of World Council of Churches member churches are based in Africa, 23 percent in Europe, and 21 percent in Asia.[6]

---

6. See "An Introduction to the World Council of Churches," *www.oikoumene.org/fileadmin/files/wcc-main/2008pdfs/wcc-introduction-2008.pdf.*

African Americans and the Episcopal Church

Partly because of its emphasis on envisioning its mission through a lens of incarnational theology, God's presence and action in the world, the Episcopal Church will always be engaged in social issues. Just as the United States was largely segregated after World War II, so was the Episcopal Church, and segregation and racism were major issues in the church in the 1950s and 1960s. In the 1960s, the Episcopal Church began to work more actively to end racism, by supporting civil rights laws and giving time and money to organizations that worked to end social inequalities. Each August 14 we remember **Jonathan Daniels,** a young European American Episcopalian martyred in the civil rights movement.

While African Americans had been attending seminaries since the 1800s, it wasn't until the 1950s that the Episcopal Church began to welcome both African Americans and whites at the same seminaries. During that decade, many of the mostly white Episcopal congregations in inner cities left the cities for the suburbs.

Some of the bishops in the Episcopal Church were black, but their congregations were likely to be black, too. Some dioceses merged black and white congregations, and in 1970 **John Burgess** was elected the first African American diocesan bishop to serve an American diocese.

Today about 3 percent of priests and 8 percent of bishops in the Episcopal Church are African American. In 2008 the Episcopal Church publicly apologized for its involvement in, and support for, the institution of slavery and for its support of segregation for years after the abolition of slavery in the United States. The Episcopal Church continues to struggle against racism and face its own complicity in racism.

Remembering difficult history is an opportunity to notice God breaking in, challenging our prejudices, that we might hope, trust, and remember...a tomorrow filled with God's dreams.

The Episcopal Church among Native Americans

The history of the Episcopal Church among Native Americans isn't a proud one. The 1606 charter of Jamestown, Virginia, called for the Church of England to convert the "infidels and savages" who "live in darkness and miserable ignorance of true knowledge." In the late 1800s, the Episcopal Church established missions among Indians of the Southwest, but rarely supported these ministries financially or permitted Native Americans to be ordained to the priesthood.

In the latter half of the twentieth century, the church began to work in earnest to respect the spirituality of Native Americans and recognize their full participation in the church. Two Native Americans — David Pendleton Oakerhater and Enmegahbowh — are celebrated for their ministry with Native Americans in the calendar of *Lesser Feasts and Fasts.* In 1977 the General Convention created Navajoland Area Mission from parts of the Dioceses of Arizona, Utah, and Rio Grande in New Mexico as a diocese of its own, serving the Navajo Nation. The General Convention of 1997 designated a Decade of Remembrance, Recognition, and Reconciliation "for welcoming Native Peoples into congregational life and developing an outreach partnership among urban Native Peoples." The church also maintains a Native American Ministries Office at its churchwide headquarters in New York City.

Role of Women

In 1889 the Episcopal Church adopted the office of female deaconate as a way for young single women to help care for the needs of the poor and sick and to train young people in the faith. But deaconesses did not have a liturgy of ordination in the Book of Common Prayer and had to resign if they married.

The Episcopal Church also revived religious orders for women. In 1845 **Anne Ayres**, a parishioner of the Church of the Holy Communion in New York City, became the first American religious sister in the Anglican tradition. But women still were not invited to leadership positions in the church.

From the 1920s to the 1950s, the number of deaconesses declined. Instead, many women interested in serving the church worked as directors of Christian education or teachers at seminaries.

In 1944 Florence Li Tim-Oi became the first woman ordained a priest in the Anglican Communion. She was ordained in Hong Kong to minister to Chinese refugees in Japanese-occupied China.

It was not until the 1960s and 1970s that women gained equal rights within the church. In 1964, deaconesses were given the right to marry and, in 1970, women could serve as lay readers and deputies to General Convention. After a resolution in 1973 to ordain women as priests, on July 29, 1974, eleven women deacons — known as the "Philadelphia eleven" — were ordained as priests by three retired bishops.

Although women may be ordained deacons and priests, it is up to each diocese whether to do so. Until recently, three dioceses in the United States refused to ordain or recognize the priesthood of women. That will likely change as those dioceses — Fort Worth, Quincy, and San Joaquin — reorganize upon the departure from the Episcopal Church of the former leadership of those dioceses.

The Most Rev. Katharine Jefferts Schori is the first woman presiding bishop.

Two years later, the General Convention changed canon law to allow women into the threefold ministry of deacon, priest, and bishop. In 1989, **Barbara Clementine Harris** became the first woman bishop in the Episcopal Church. In 2006, the General Convention elected **Katharine Jefferts Schori** as presiding bishop of the Episcopal Church. By April 2008, the Episcopal Church had elected fifteen women bishops.

Ministry of Youth

The Episcopal Church recognizes the ministry of youth as necessary for a lively and vibrant community. In 1982, the Episcopal Church held the first National Episcopal Youth Event, a triennial gathering of over a thousand youth from throughout the Episcopal Church, including Latin American and Caribbean dioceses, and international participants. Every three years, young people from across the country and around the world gather for a week of worship, learning, and fellowship. Young people themselves design and plan the services and lead music and worship. Each of the Episcopal Church's nine provinces also sends two young people to participate in the Official Youth Presence at General Convention.

THE EPISCOPAL CHURCH TODAY

The Episcopal Church today has over seven thousand congregations and missions and 2.2 million active baptized members, about 770,000 of whom regularly attend Sunday worship. About 60 percent of the laity and 30 percent of clergy are women.

The Episcopal Church still works hard for greater unity among all churches and takes social issues just as seriously as ever. The Episcopal Church maintains an Office of Government Relations in Washington, D.C., to advocate for the poor, the environment, and other social issues. Internationally, the Episcopal Church cooperates with Anglican churches to provide relief to those in Africa suffering with HIV/AIDS. The Episcopal Church has established achieving the Millennium Development Goals (MDGs) as its first priority.

The MDGs are eight goals agreed to by the nations of the world to halve extreme poverty in the world by 2015. A grassroots organization, Episcopalians for Global Reconciliation (*www.e4gr.org*) is committed to encouraging the church to do its part in fulfilling these goals.

The expanding role of women in the church and differing beliefs about social issues, including homosexuality, over four decades, as well as the confirmation by General Convention of the election of an openly gay priest, **V. Gene Robinson**, as bishop of the Diocese of New Hampshire, has occasioned controversy within the Episcopal Church and has strained relationships between the Episcopal Church and some churches in the wider Anglican Communion. Nevertheless, the Episcopal Church proclaims at every baptism the promise to "strive for justice and peace and respect the dignity of every human being."

In the early 2000s the Episcopal Church actively worked toward peace in the Middle East, eliminating global poverty, supporting economic development, providing voice and assistance to the oppressed in the Sudan, and advocating on behalf of those suffering with HIV/AIDS. While the Episcopal Church prefers nonviolent approaches to conflict, it also affirms that people must discern their individual participation in the military.

The Episcopal Church, which has its history in the Church of England and counts George Washington as one of its early members, has traditionally been a church that welcomes diversity. About 5 percent of Episcopalians are black, 1 percent are Latino, and 1 percent are Asian/Pacific Islander.[7] Our buildings and our styles of worship vary greatly, but we are a people bound by a shared faith, common ministry, and common prayer.

---

7. "Episcopal Congregations Overview: Findings from the 2008 Faith Communities Today Survey," *www.episcopalchurch.org/documents/Episcopal_Overview_FACT_2008.pdf*

✝ TRANSFORMING QUESTIONS

1. **Be Attentive:** Select a contemporary issue facing the Episcopal Church today. What do you believe about the issue? Have you prejudged the issue or those who espouse one position or another?

2. **Be Intelligent:** Identify an experience that relates to your belief. How does this experience affirm or challenge your belief? What other understandings are possible?

3. **Be Reasonable:** What do others believe about this issue? You may want to confirm your understanding with others. What new information or perspectives do these other positions bring to your own beliefs?

4. **Be Responsible:** Do your new insights suggest that you might act differently?

5. **Be in Love Transformed:** What might you do in the future to invite others to share different perspectives on an issue?

Chapter Five

Faith: Whom Do We Trust?

BE NOT AFRAID

She screamed. God would get me for the smiling sinner I am. She was hawking literature near a table laden with posters proclaiming that judgment was at hand. "Be afraid," the bold strokes of the images proclaimed. A vengeful God will have his day.

Religious rants arouse my reactivity, to say nothing of occupational embarrassment. Might someone think she and I are in the same business, just on different sides of the street? To allay seething anger within, I smiled. That wasn't enough. I had to look at her and slowly shake my head.

It was the reaction she sought. She singled me out among the fast walkers in the New York City subway corridor near the Port Authority. Raging threats of God's wrath, she followed my wife and me. She made thirty seconds seem like ten minutes. I had given her an opportunity to bounce her caricature of God off hundreds of feet of the underground tiles. We didn't look back at this true believer.

The irony is that variations of "be not afraid" and "you are loved" appear throughout the Bible she uses to scare people.

If you have lived your life without the experience of fear or guilt prompted by messages from within or outside yourself that "God will get you" for your sins, you are fortunate. You may have avoided the pain of that caricature of God delivered by many multimedia evangelists and, perhaps, even your family, your friends, or your church.

Somehow you may have escaped. You may have had the personal security and self-worth not to submit yourself to this rack. You may think you escaped simply by not believing in God. In your heart and mind, however, you continue to journey along a path to authenticity that has meaning beyond yourself.

The single most difficult Christian belief is not that the one true God is a Trinitarian community, nor that God became one of us, nor that God raised Jesus from the dead, nor that we too will be raised. The most difficult Christian belief is to trust that God forgives and loves us before we repent.

God's good news, as I understand it, is that God loves and forgives us, while we are yet sinners, not because we repent. Rather, we become repentant and transformed because God has forgiven and loved us. I rely on this radical, incredible love of God.

This is not the understanding proposed by those who — with whatever religious intent — attempt to manipulate us into thinking that in order to be "saved," we must take the initiative.

The evidence leading toward the understanding that God takes the initiative — a rumor of angels, as Peter Berger put it in his forty-year-old book about "signals" of transcendence — is there for anyone willing to search their own experience and the scriptures, without making the Bible an idol. Those who seek fear, however, will find it. Fear is best ignored in favor of what is found in the major themes.

I paraphrase, from Isaiah: "Be not afraid, for I have redeemed you. I have called you by name, you are mine. Should you pass through the sea, I will be there with you; or through rivers, you will not drown. . . . For you are precious in my eyes, and honored, and I love you. . . . Be not afraid, for I am with you."

We need to hear the major themes again and again. In the mirror, we need to see one who has been forgiven and is loved.

"Rarely will anyone die for a righteous person," Paul writes in his Letter to the Romans, "though perhaps for a good person someone might actually dare to die. God proves his love for us in that while we were yet sinners Christ died for us." While we were yet sinners.

Why do we find that so difficult to believe? Perhaps because of how difficult it is to imagine that we might act that way toward others. We can't conceive, Graham Greene has written in *Brighton Rock*, of "the appalling strangeness of the mercy of God."

"It is I, be not afraid," Jesus said to his disciples as he walked on the water through a storm toward their battered boat.

"For the wonders that astound us, for the truths that still confound us," some of us have sung, "most of all that love has found us, thanks be to God."   *— B.L.*

◆ ◆ ◆

Jesus said to him, "Go; your faith has made you well." Immediately he regained his sight and followed him on the way. (Mark 10:52)

In a few words, "Go; your faith has made you well," Jesus healed blind Bartimaeus. Without sight the world was threatening, dangerous, limiting, and full of fear. Blind Bartimaeus made a life begging at the side of the road, taking more than giving. But, sensing that Jesus was near, Bartimaeus cried out, "Have mercy." Jesus answered, "What do you want me to do for you?" "My teacher, let me see again," he said. Jesus then proclaimed, "Go; your faith has made you well."

Bartimaeus's faith gave him a new *way of seeing,* and it showed him a world filled with light, hope, and possibility. In this new world with God's love, Bartimaeus need not be afraid. Perhaps Bartimaeus had endured taunts like those of the woman preaching fear of God's vengeance in the subway corridor. We do not know. We do know that Bartimaeus was healed. God loved Bartimaeus, and he was so changed by this new way of seeing that he got up immediately and followed Jesus. Just like that, he became a disciple.

Our faith too is a new way of seeing. Through faith we see the world as a place in which God blesses us and invites us to respond with loving actions. We express how we experience God's love in our statements of belief.

STATEMENTS OF FAITH

We have three statements of faith in the Episcopal Church — the Nicene Creed, the Apostles' Creed, and the Athanasian Creed. We say the Nicene Creed during Holy Eucharist and the Apostles' Creed during the Service of Baptism and when we say the "Daily Office" of Morning Prayer and Evening Prayer in the Book of Common Prayer. You can find the Athanasian Creed among historical documents in the Book of Common Prayer (pages 864–65).

> Have you encountered someone proclaiming a gospel of fear and judgment as Bill did in the subway? How did you or others around you react? How does this experience contrast with that of Bartimaeus?

These creeds are ancient statements of belief that grew out of questions and disputes in the early years of the church. Who exactly are Jesus and the Holy Spirit? Is the Holy Spirit also divine? Is Jesus both divine and human? Is belief in God the Father, Son, and Holy Spirit, belief in one God? How are the Father, Son, and Holy Spirit related? Church councils in Nicea and Chalcedon, towns in present-day Turkey, met during the fourth and fifth centuries to address these questions, and in response wrote the Nicene Creed. The Nicene Creed begins with the word "We" because it is a statement of faith by a community.

The **Apostles' Creed** developed from the answers to the questions the church asked candidates for baptism in the early years of Christianity. Those questions are:

Do you believe in God the Father?

Do you believe in Jesus Christ, the Son of God?

Do you believe in God the Holy Spirit?

Candidates for baptism — or their godparents — continue to answer these very same questions today. The Apostles' Creed is a personal statement of belief, so it begins with the word "I" — "I believe in God, the Father almighty."

THE APOSTLES' CREED

Take a minute or two to read the Apostles' Creed slowly.

> I believe in God, the Father almighty,
>   creator of heaven and earth.
>
> I believe in Jesus Christ, his only Son, our Lord.
>   He was conceived by the power of the Holy Spirit
>   and born of the Virgin Mary.
>   He suffered under Pontius Pilate,
>   was crucified, died, and was buried.
>   He descended to the dead.
>   On the third day he rose again.
>   He ascended into heaven,
>   and is seated at the right hand of the Father.
>   He will come again to judge the living and the dead.
>
> I believe in the Holy Spirit,
>   the holy catholic Church,
>   the communion of saints,
>   the forgiveness of sins,
>   the resurrection of the body,
>   and the life everlasting.

Belief

The Apostles' Creed begins with the words "I believe in God." When we say "I believe in God," we aren't asserting that God exists. We are saying that we have a relationship with God. It's just like saying to someone you love, "I believe in you." Remember from chapter 2, the word "creed" comes from the Latin word *credere*, meaning "to give one's heart to or put one's trust in." So when we proclaim our belief in God, what we're really saying is, "I give my heart to God." What a difference this makes! By giving our hearts to God we are entering into a relationship of trust. The creeds are statements about the God we love and trust.

Say the Apostles' Creed, substituting the words "I love" for the words "I believe." How does this change your understanding?

The Trinity

The Apostles' Creed (like the Nicene Creed) has three parts: I believe in God..., I believe in Jesus Christ..., I believe in the Holy Spirit.... Three persons in one: Father, Son, and Holy Spirit. We call God who exists in three eternal, distinct, and equal persons **Trinity**. The word "trinity" comes from two Latin words — *tri* meaning three and *unitas* meaning unity. God's nature is three persons united in one God.

The triquetra is a symbol of the Trinity.

The doctrine of the Trinity was developed early in the church's history and has a very specific meaning. We believe that the three persons that are One God are *one, equal,* and *coeternal.*

One. Try thinking about the Trinity as similar to the parts of time: Time is composed of past, present, and future. Each is distinct from the other, yet each is an expression of the same concept, that is, time. The past does not represent one kind of time, the present another, and the future still another. They are *one.* Likewise, God the Father, God the Son, and God the Holy Spirit are each distinct persons, yet each is God.

Equal. Past, present, and future each represents a different aspect of the same time. One isn't more important than the other, but you can understand one only alongside the others. You cannot, for example, understand the past without also knowing about both the present and the future. Suppose you went to church on Sunday. On the next day, Monday, you can say that your going to church happened in the past. How do you know it was in the past? Because you know it is an event that happened before the present day, Monday. You see, you know the past only in relation to the present. The same is true for the future. All times — present, past, and future — are equal and are known only in relation to the other. This represents their *equality.* In the same way, God the Father, God the Son, and God the Holy Spirit are equal persons as One God. The way we understand the Son, for example, helps us understand the Father and the Holy Spirit, too.

Coeternal. We can't really understand the time without a past, present, and future — those three elements are **coeternal**. That is, all three are part of one;

they have been so always and together will always be a part of our concept of time. The Son and the Holy Spirit were with God the Father before creation, are with God now, and will be with God to the end of time. In much the same way, the three persons, God the Father, God the Son, and God the Holy Spirit, have existed and will exist together for all time.

WHAT THE WORDS IN THE APOSTLES' CREED MEAN

When praying any creed, be attentive to the words and only those words, not to particular understandings that you or others may lay on the words. Recognize that people and churches have laid more than one understanding on creedal statements and that the Episcopal Church does not require that you choose one or another of those understandings in order to be an Episcopalian.

I believe in God

We begin with the first person of the Trinity — God the Father. We're affirming that God is real, that there is a wonderful and magnificent "other" to whom we're faithful, in whom we trust, and who is intimately concerned with each of us — our well-being and our relationships with other people and all creation. But even more than that, we're proclaiming that we love God, we give our hearts to God, and we want to have a relationship with God.

the Father almighty,
creator of heaven and earth.

We don't believe in just any God. The God we love adopted us as daughters and sons and enters human history again and again with mighty acts that continually reconcile us to God. We believe in the God who made all things, both in heaven and on earth, who is the source of all things, everywhere.

God as Father is just one image that Christians use to express their experience of God. Throughout the Bible, God is described in many ways. God is described as both male and female. In Isaiah 66:13, for example, God is depicted as a mother who comforts her child. God is described as nature. In Psalm 28, for example, the psalmist calls God "my Rock." The prayers we use during church services express many images for God: God as ruler of the universe, fountain of life, source of goodness, holy Lord, shield and armor of light, holy wisdom, and giver of life. These images acknowledge that God reveals God's self in many ways. Any one image cannot adequately describe God.

Acknowledging God — and our loving relationship with him — makes us see the world in a totally different way. When the Israelites faced a hostile wilderness as they journeyed out of Egypt and wondered how they'd ever find their way, God guided them with a cloud by day and a pillar of fire by night. When they had nothing to eat, God gave them manna from heaven — enough for their daily needs. When they were thirsty, God led them to a rock that Moses struck, ordering it to gush with water to quench their thirst.

In the Christian scriptures, Jesus continued to show us new ways of seeing the world. The poor, he said, will receive the kingdom of God, the hungry will be satisfied, the sad will laugh, and mourners will be comforted. When we see the world the way Jesus sees it, we look at the world a lot differently. Later in the chapter, we'll explore how believing in God changes our actions.

I believe in Jesus Christ, his only Son, our Lord.

We proclaim our belief in the second person of the Trinity — Jesus Christ. By saying "I believe in Jesus Christ," we're doing more than acknowledging that somebody named Jesus lived in a little country in the Middle East two thousand years ago. Instead, we're committing our lives to this Jesus and becoming his followers, or disciples. We're committing ourselves to the law of Moses (the Ten Commandments) and to the new commandment of Jesus: to love our neighbor as ourselves.

The second part of this phrase (his only Son) affirms that Jesus is the perfect human image of the Divine. Just as we reflect our own parents, Jesus reflects God. His life and ministry show us the essence of God, which is love. We call Jesus "our Lord" because we know he brings us to God. In the Gospel according to John, Jesus says, "I am the way, and the truth, and the life. No one comes to the Father except through me" (John 14:6). Christians who acknowledge Jesus as their way to the Father need not believe that God does not relate to those who commit to God in ways other than Christian.

He was conceived by the power of the Holy Spirit and born of the Virgin Mary.

This is a strong statement! It says that we believe Jesus is both human and divine. By entering our world as a human being, God entered history and became a person just like you and me. God became one of us. Jesus was born, just like us, into a human family, and grew up in that family. The Gospels focus on Jesus' public ministry as an adult and don't say very much at all about Jesus' youth. This shouldn't surprise us. They aren't modern biographies. They are proclamations of the good news that God's kingdom is near.

But the Gospels do tell us lots of things about what Jesus was like. Like us, Jesus slept, ate, laughed, and cried. Like us, Jesus faced temptations. Like us, Jesus faced times of weakness and asked God to take away his troubles. Like us, Jesus needed his closest friends for support. Like us, Jesus felt pain. Jesus was subjected to the great suffering on the cross.

Our belief that Jesus was God in the flesh is called the **Incarnation**. The Word became flesh and lived among us. We say the words "Virgin Mary" both to emphasize Jesus' humanity and to connect Jesus with the ancient prophecy in Isaiah 7:14: "Therefore the Lord himself will give you a sign. Look, the young woman is with child and shall bear a son, and shall name him Immanuel [meaning God is with us]."

> The words "born of the Virgin Mary" proclaim our belief that Jesus did not simply take on the appearance of a man, but was truly human, as well as truly divine. The scandal of our faith is that God redeemed creation by entering into it.

Jesus was also fully divine. Nothing separated Jesus from God. Jesus expressed the love of God in his life by healing the sick, forgiving sins, mending broken relationships, turning away from evil, and calling everyone back to friendship with God. We don't mean that Jesus was just a man who led a good life, but that God the Father lived completely in Jesus. God took on human nature in Jesus.

He suffered under Pontius Pilate,

It might seem odd to mention Pontius Pilate in a statement of belief about God. He got a bad rap in the Bible as the Roman leader who questioned Jesus at his trial and condemned him to death on the cross. So why include him in the creed? Mentioning Pontius Pilate by name sets Jesus squarely into human history. Pontius Pilate was governor of Judea, an ancient region in Palestine that was part of the Roman Empire, and from 26 to 36 C.E., the time of Jesus' crucifixion, it included the city of Jerusalem. His rule is recorded by the Jewish historian Josephus, who lived shortly after Jesus. God became flesh at a specific time and place.

The cross is a central Christian symbol.

was crucified, died, and was buried. He descended to the dead.

Jesus really did suffer and die as a human on the cross. Through Jesus, God chose to suffer and die as one of us. We say he descended to the dead not necessarily to say that Jesus literally went to a place where the dead resided, but that God offers salvation through Jesus to all people — to the living and those who had already died before Jesus came to the earth. Death is not the last word for anyone. God offers freedom from death, or salvation, to *all* people.

On the third day he rose again.

After Jesus died a number of women came to the tomb where Jesus was laid to anoint his body with perfumes and oils. But they were amazed to find that the tomb was empty. An angel told the women that Jesus had risen from the dead, or resurrected. They ran to tell Jesus' closest friends, the disciples. For forty days, the risen Jesus revealed himself to the disciples, who recognized him whenever they shared a meal together.

By conquering death, Jesus opened the way for eternal life. "Eternal life and salvation" has a variety of meanings. Eternal life and salvation means a life without physical or emotional suffering and a life where our sins are forgiven. We cannot experience salvation completely as human beings living on earth. But through our faith in God and with God's help we can make choices that lessen human suffering and demonstrate God's love to others.

Because Jesus rose from the dead, we no longer have to live completely separated from God. And just as he revealed himself to the disciples, Jesus continues to reveal himself to us through the Eucharist, the meal Christians share together, and through the loving actions of people toward one another and creation. Death did not end the story.

> The resurrection of Jesus is at the heart of what it means to be a Christian. Through Jesus' resurrection we are made a new creation and given a way of eternal life.

He ascended into heaven, and is seated at the right hand of the Father.

We believe that Jesus dwells with the Father just as someday we will, too. The words "seated at the right hand" don't mean that Jesus is literally sitting next to God on God's right. It is a way of saying that Jesus shares in the authority and power of God as ruler of all creation.

He will come again to judge the living and the dead.

Jesus came to proclaim the good news of God: "The time is fulfilled, and the kingdom of God has come near; repent, and believe in the good news" (Mark 1:15). God created the world and rules the world today. What we mean by ruling the world is that God has a purpose and order for the world. We are to love our neighbors as ourselves. We are to take care of the earth and all living creatures. God sent Jesus to show us the way to live according to God's will and to offer the healing we need to love ourselves, others, and creation. We also look forward to a time when we are no longer separated from God and are completely within God's will. We look for the time when our relationship with God is completely restored, when we meet God face-to-face, so to speak.

I believe in the Holy Spirit,

The **Holy Spirit** is the third person of the Trinity — God's power and presence in our past, our present, and our future. The Holy Spirit is God at work in the world and the church — from the beginning of time to eternity. The Holy Spirit is the breath over nothingness at creation, the manna from heaven that fed the Israelites in the wilderness, the words of God at the start of Jesus' ministry saying, "This is my Son, the Beloved, with whom I am well pleased" (Matthew 3:17). The Holy Spirit is the rush of violent

The descending dove is a symbol of the Holy Spirit.

wind at Pentecost when the apostles began to spread the good news of Jesus in other languages. The Holy Spirit is the person of the Trinity that strengthens, nourishes, and sustains us. Through the Holy Spirit, we live in Christ and Christ lives in us. Through the Holy Spirit, we bring Christ's joy, peace, and justice into the world.

the holy catholic Church,

"Catholic" is another word for universal, or worldwide. When we say that we believe in the **catholic** church, we mean we support one universal faith community, all those who believe in Jesus. This church began with Jesus. It was founded when the Holy Spirit descended upon the apostles on Pentecost. And it continues today. We, like those baptized at the founding of the church, devote ourselves "to the apostles' teaching and fellowship, to the breaking of bread, and to the prayers" (Acts 2:42).

the communion of saints,

We are each one of many members of the body of Christ. The word "saints" here means a community of faithful people who believe in God and Jesus Christ. When we are initiated into the life of the church at baptism, we become a saint with a lowercase "s." Affirming our membership in this community means that we're related in our faith with all other members of the body of Christ, or the church. We care for that relationship through worship, prayer, and serving one another.

the forgiveness of sins,

No matter what we do wrong, God wants to restore our friendship and forgives us even before we ask. At baptism, we — or our parents and sponsors — renounce evil and turn to Jesus Christ as our Savior. But inevitably we miss the mark and fail to live up to our baptismal promises by things we do — and by things we don't do. Our actions, as well as our refusal to do what God calls us to do, bring evil into the world, and sometimes we fail to do what God asks us. So again and again we need to turn away from evil, say we're sorry, and ask for God's forgiveness. We can be confident that God will always forgive us.

the resurrection of the body, and the life everlasting.

We believe that God will raise us in our entirety to a new life with God. Because we are living members of the body of Christ — the church — we share in Jesus' resurrection. Just as Jesus conquered sin, suffering, and death, we will no longer experience pain or suffering. We will be resurrected in perfection by God and, as resurrected people, we will be united with God, living in perfect joy and peace with one another, loving God and each other in a way that is not possible now. Ultimately, nothing — not sin, not suffering that we know now on earth, not even death — will separate us from the love of God.

FAITH AS SEEING AND RESPONDING

Bartimaeus's faith opened up his eyes and made him jump up and follow Jesus. Notice those two actions: faith gave sight and sight prompted a response. The same is true for our faith. Our faith means we see the world within a relationship with God. And we respond in ways that maintain our relationship with God and the world. Like Bartimaeus, we're called to follow.

We say we believe in — give our hearts to — God almighty. What we see is a God who is with us, loves us, and takes care of us. God is at the center of our lives and we promise to live according to God's will. We say we believe in — give our hearts to — Jesus. What we see is a world in which God knows us intimately — our pain, our joy, and our fears — because through Jesus he became one of us. Jesus still shows us signs of the kingdom of God that is filled with life, joy, plenty, and justice. In return, we promise to be disciples of Jesus, to be signs of the kingdom of God today. We say we believe in — give our hearts to — the Holy Spirit. That means we see a world in which God is actively offering us forgiveness, giving us what we need to grow, and guiding us to make good choices. We respond by welcoming God's guidance, accepting God's forgiveness, and seeking God's will for our lives. We do this by taking the time to pray each day, offering God our questions, and asking for guidance. We do this by inviting God into our decisions and continuing to ask ourselves whether what we are doing is sharing the love that God gives us.

Believing changes how we see things and how we respond to the world. Belief without action is not belief.

How Do We Know How to Respond?

Remember, our relationship with God is a covenant relationship. The stories of the Hebrew scriptures (Old Testament), the life and ministry of Jesus, and the promises we made at baptism tell us about how to live into that sacred covenant. When God started a covenant with the Israelites, God promised to be their God, guiding them and giving them land, food, and drink. In response, God required the people to be faithful, to do justice, to love mercy, and to walk humbly with their God. Christians refer to the sacred covenant God established with the Israelites as the **Old Covenant**. Think of the word "old" here as a term of respect. It does not mean that this covenant is no longer life-giving or relevant.

As part of the covenant with the Israelites, God gave the Ten Commandments to show what it means to live within the covenant. You can read them in Exodus 20:1–17 and also in Deuteronomy 5:6–21. The first four commandments define our relationship with God. We worship one God. We honor God through love and respect and by putting God first. The last six commandments define our relationship with others. To be faithful to our relationships with others means we act in ways that show honor, love, and respect for all life.

Jesus came into the world to fulfill the laws that God gave to the Israelites. That is, Jesus fulfilled God's laws by perfectly loving God and loving his neighbors as he loved himself. And more, through his resurrection, Jesus fulfilled the laws by offering us forgiveness for all the times we disobey God's laws. Jesus started a new covenant, a new relationship for us with God. In the **New Covenant**, Jesus promises us the kingdom of God, a life marked by joy, community, plenty, and justice. In the New Covenant, Christ calls us to respond in love by keeping his laws, especially the following two **Great Commandments:**

"You shall love the Lord your God with all your heart and with all your soul, and with all your mind."

And

"You shall love your neighbor as yourself." (Matthew 22:35–40)

Notice how these two Great Commandments follow the Ten Commandments. The first commandment is about loving God while the second is about loving others. To live within the covenant relationship with God, our every action should reflect our love for God, self, and neighbor. The Catechism in the Book of Common Prayer (page 847) offers a specific guide on how to do this.

Honoring our relationship with God means that we:

- love and obey God and bring others to know God;

- put nothing in the place of God;

- show God respect in thought, word, and deed; and

- and set aside regular times for worship, prayer, and the study of God's ways.

We choose to take these actions as free responses to our loving God. Imagine meeting a person who brings out the best in you, makes you laugh, and who stays by your side. We introduce that friend to our other friends, and we always make time to be together.

These first four actions place God at the center of our lives. They help us to know God's generous love. Knowing that love, we can see the goodness that God wants for the world. By taking time to love God and putting God at the center, we allow God to draw us toward actions that share God's love. These actions will be to:

- love, honor, and help our neighbors;

- respect life and do things that bring peace to the world;

- respect ourselves and our bodies;

- be honest and fair in all that we do;

- speak the truth;

- honor the life and gifts of others.

God loves all creation. When we join God's kingdom we also love all creation as God loves us — without reservation. We take care of the earth and everything in it. We live honestly. We usually think of rules as a nuisance, but they're really a way of freedom because they help people live happily with one another. The Old Covenant and the New Covenant show us the way to have good relationships with God and with others.

Breaking Relationship

Following God's will isn't always easy. Sometimes we fall short of doing God's will. That is, we **sin**. The Catechism defines sin as "seeking of our own will instead of the will of God, thus distorting our relationship with God, with other people, and with all creation" (Book of Common Prayer, page 848).

When we sin we are breaking our promises to God and our relationship with God and one another. We often put ourselves — not God — first. Every day, things that are bad tempt us away from the love of God. This evil takes away our faith and takes away our ability to know God's love and see the possibilities for a world filled with God's love.

We cannot promise not to sin, but we can promise to acknowledge when we have acted wrongly, seek forgiveness, and with God's help promise to make right choices.

Asking for Forgiveness

What if we break our promises to God and one another? At our baptism, we (or our parents and godparents) promised "to persevere in resisting evil, and whenever [we] fall into sin, repent and return to the Lord." We didn't promise to be perfect or never to sin; that would be a promise we could never keep. We promised that when we sin we will acknowledge what we'd done, turn away from sin, and turn toward God by asking forgiveness from God and those we've hurt. We promised to restore a right relationship with God and with other people. We can seek forgiveness in many ways. We can ask God's forgiveness anytime at all. We also confess our sins as a community during our Sunday worship. And we can receive the sacrament called Reconciliation of a Penitent, confessing our sins privately to a priest and receiving absolution, or forgiveness. Chapter 10 explores this sacrament.

PUTTING YOUR FAITH INTO PRACTICE

Like Bartimaeus, we see the world in a whole new way when our eyes are opened up by faith. With our every action, we try to follow the two Great Commandments of Jesus, and our baptismal promises help us do that. Our actions are the ways we put into practice the faith that's in our hearts.

✠ TRANSFORMING QUESTIONS

1. **Be Attentive:** Identify a time when you felt embraced by God's love. Describe the event. What happened? Who was present? What was said or done?

2. **Be Intelligent:** How does it feel to be embraced by God's love? What were you thinking at the time? What do your thoughts and feelings suggest about what it means to be embraced by God's love?

3. **Be Reasonable:** Share your story with a companion and invite your companion to share with you a story about feeling God's embrace. What do your stories have in common? How are they different? What do the similarities and differences mean about God's embrace?

4. **Be Responsible:** What are you able to challenge yourself to do as a result of God's embrace?

5. **Be in Love Transformed:** What do you need to give up to take up that challenge? Pray for the grace to do so.

Chapter Six

Navigating the Church

A TROUBLING CALL

When searching for a chosen people, God went to several nations to see how they would respond. One spoke of its wealth; another, its philosophical systems; another, its power. God also asked a small group of slaves. They were not wealthy. They had not developed philosophical systems. They were also oppressed. "If you choose us, we'll tell our children stories about everything you ever do for us." God said, "Yes!" God loves a good story.

Israel prays in Psalm 78: "That which we have heard and known, and what our forefathers have told us, we will not hide from their children."

God loves to hear our stories; and, as theologian and storyteller John Shea says, "God loves to tell his own. Quite simply, we are the story God tells."

We are God's story especially when, gathered in faith communities, we live into God's strong verbs: repent, be, do, give, forgive, go, sow, pray, judge not, fear not, feed the hungry, clothe the naked, heal the sick, welcome the stranger, visit the imprisoned, proclaim good news, love God with all your heart, love your neighbor as yourself, love your enemies, be reconciled, find your life by losing it for my sake, make disciples.

The perennial Christian strategy of Acts 2:42 — "They devoted themselves to the apostles' teaching and fellowship, to the breaking of bread and the prayers" — has been paraphrased as (1) gather the folks; (2) break the bread; (3) share the stories.

Though it is crucial that the stories be told far beyond the close quarters of churches, the true story upon which our lives as Christians are based — the life, dying, and new life of Jesus Christ — is rehearsed again and again where the folks are gathered to break the bread. Re-membering our subversive story in our faith communities is at the heart of Passover and Eucharist.

"The only necessities for a gathered Episcopal church," Diocese of Bethlehem bishop Paul Marshall has written, "are people, a priest, a Bible, a prayer book, some bread, and some wine. Everything else is a cultural decision." Bishop Marshall also suggests an effective question to help navigate the church: Is your church helping you to grow up?

"A grown-up and healthy religion is not solely concerned with making people feel good about themselves, and certainly does not dabble in making them feel superior to others," he writes. "It does not reinforce feelings of persecution and victimhood, but asks its adherents how they will put their awareness of their own value and purpose into practice as they encounter other, equally valuable, people.

"Is your spiritual or faith community helping you grow up? Keep track of the messages you receive from it in the next month in word, print, image, or act. How many messages move you beyond valuing self to valuing others (as something other than potential converts)? How many messages encourage suspicion or mistrust of others? How many messages keep you focused on the past? How many messages encourage you to move into a creative future?"

There's a story about a troubled teenager named Jesus. His mother, Mary, took him to a monastery, to a monk who had a reputation as a teacher and healer. The monk asked Jesus what was troubling him. "God," Jesus said. "God is making me wonder about things. About who I am. About what I might do. I don't know why."

The monk suggested that Mary allow Jesus to stay with him for a while. He convinced Jesus that God would not trouble a young man in this way. The teenage Jesus was healed. He returned with his mother to Nazareth where he lived a relatively happy life as a carpenter—and died of old age.

Commenting on this story he heard from Jesuit peace activist Daniel Berrigan, Tom Roberts, now of the *National Catholic Reporter,* then a journalist/columnist with the old Bethlehem (Pennsylvania) *Globe-Times*, wrote: "Christian communities should stand as signs of contradiction in any age. If they don't, then either the kingdom promised is here in all its fulfillment or we're doing something wrong."

The remedy is God's, Roberts continued. Nevertheless, "God's action takes us into account. We live at the intersection of very mysterious freedoms, God's and our own. …Never did those freedoms brush against each other more intimately than with the life of that wild holy that began two thousand years ago in another Bethlehem."

All we have been given—energy, talent, time, money—has been given us for the sake of God's remedy, the kingdom. God's remedy begins with God's troubling call. May we not tame its totality simply for the illusion of a relatively happy life.

—B.L.

◆ ◆ ◆

As you read this chapter about the structure of the Episcopal Church today, do ask yourself, "Is your church helping you to grow up?" "Is the church standing as a sign of contradiction in this age?" Knowing about how the church works will help you explore these questions.

ONE, HOLY, CATHOLIC, AND APOSTOLIC

As you read in chapter 4 the Episcopal Church in the United States was established in 1789. About seventeen hundred years or so earlier, on Pentecost, the church was born.

As we say each Sunday with the words of the Nicene Creed, the church that was born on Pentecost is "the one, holy, catholic, and apostolic church." By *one* we mean that the church is one body with Christ as its head. All denominations are not the same, but all worship the same God. By *holy* we mean that the Holy Spirit dwells among us and continues to guide us in representing Christ in the world. By **catholic** (lowercase c) we mean universal. Our faith is a faith for all people and for all time. God intended the church to be for all nations, for the wealthy and poor alike, for both men and women, and for people of every social class and level of education. In the Prayers of the People each week, we pray for the whole church, all Christian people.

> The oneness of the church is about how the church is the community of those who are led to the one place at the Father's heart where he can be known, where he can be seen.   —Rowan Williams[8]

The church is **apostolic** because the church continues in the teaching and community that the apostles began in the years after Jesus' death and resurrection. Just after the baptism of thousands on Pentecost, the writer of the Acts of the Apostles tells us that the newly baptized "devoted themselves to the apostles' teaching and fellowship, to the breaking of bread and the prayers." The church continues those central actions and has an unbroken history from its birth on Pentecost to the present day.

As a whole and in its parts, the church is the community of people who, at baptism, renounced evil and turned to Jesus Christ as their Savior. The church is a people who believe in God the Father, God the Son, and God the Holy Spirit. The Episcopal Church is part of the one, holy, catholic, and apostolic church.

It is neither attentive nor intelligent to suggest, as some occasionally have, that the Episcopal Church was founded by Henry VIII, thereby cutting the link between today's Episcopal Church and the church founded by Jesus

---

8. "One Holy Catholic and Apostolic Church," archbishop's address to the 3rd Global South to South Encounter, Ain al Sukhna, Egypt, October 28, 2005.

Christ. Be attentive to and try to understand the clues within the structure and worship of the Episcopal Church that suggest continuation with the church of Jesus Christ and the Christians of the early centuries.

A LIVING ORGANISM

The homes of bee colonies are a beautiful arrangement of hexagonal cells made to fit perfectly together. More amazing than the beauty of their homes is their behavior. Bees act in a colony as if they are a single organism. Each has a specific role to play that keeps the entire community healthy. One queen bee lays eggs all day. Depending on their stage of life, worker bees take care of larvae (the newly hatched bees), clean house, or forage for food. Drones mate with virgin queens from other colonies to pass along their colony's genes. The colony's survival depends on each bee fulfilling its duties. Bees are so committed to their colony that they will give up their lives to protect it. A honey bee dies soon after it stings.

Just like a bee hive, the church is a living organism with thousands of members, each with a specific role to play. When working well, the hive acts as one with one mission: "to restore all people to unity with God and each other in Christ." The church needs each of its members to carry out this mission, and it needs these members to act in a coordinated way.

YOU AND THE OTHER MINISTERS

Baptism is full initiation into the body of Christ, which makes you, no matter how young or old, whatever your profession or personal history, a *full* member of the church. Nothing more is needed to complete your membership. You don't need to pass a test. At your baptism you were already marked as Christ's own forever. As a member of the body of Christ, you're also a *minister* of the church; you're called to serve others on behalf of Christ. This broad definition of "minister" may surprise you. Most people reserve the word "minister" for the ordained. But because each member of the church is called to live out the promises made at baptism, each member has a ministry and is a minister of the church.

The ministers of the church include laypersons, bishops, priests, and deacons. While all ministers share the basic ministry of representing Jesus and his church, each person is called in a different way to fulfill that ministry. **Laypersons** find their ministry working and acting out in the world as students, workers, parents, community activists, and so on. The remaining three ministries are ordained ministries.

We discuss ordained ministries in chapter 10. In the next chapter, we explore the ministry of the laity. Here is a brief explanation of each. Bishops serve as apostles, chief priests, and pastors of a diocese. Priests lead parishes as a pastor to the people. Deacons perform special ministries of serving the needs of others, especially the poor, the sick, and the suffering. Deacons also assist priests or bishops in worship. Laypersons, bishops, priests, and deacons are all ministers in the Episcopal Church.

THE EPISCOPAL CHURCH (TEC)

The Episcopal Church comprises about 2.3 million members in just over seven thousand churches and missions, three hundred bishops, fourteen thousand priests, and nearly two thousand deacons throughout the United States, Latin America, the Caribbean, Taiwan, and Europe. Latin American and Caribbean countries included in the Episcopal Church are Colombia, the Dominican Republic, Ecuador, Haiti, Honduras, Puerto Rico, the Virgin Islands, and Venezuela. The Episcopal Church in Europe comprises American churches whose membership is made up mostly of Americans living abroad, for example those in the military, in business, or studying in a foreign country.

> Episcopalians understand themselves as both Protestant and Catholic — Protestant because they worship in their own language, use a Book of Common Prayer, and rely on scripture, reason, and tradition to interpret the Bible; Catholic because they uphold the faith of the early church through the sacraments and creeds.

The Episcopal Church affirms a principle of comprehensiveness, considers itself to be a church of the radical center, Catholic and Reformed, at once fully Catholic and Protestant. "While applying this principle of comprehensiveness is extremely difficult to do in practice," writes John Westerhoff in *A People Called Episcopalians*, "the struggle to do so is an important aspect of our tradition."[9] Nevertheless, the Episcopal Church is commonly counted among Protestant churches (that is, distinct from the Roman Catholic and the Eastern Orthodox churches). While just over half of Americans are members of a Protestant church, 1 percent are members of the Episcopal Church.

9. John H. Westerhoff, *A People Called Episcopalians* (Harrisburg, Pa.: Morehouse Publishing, 1994), 21.

Parallels between
the United States Government
and the Episcopal Church

Nation . . . . Episcopal Church
President . . . . Presiding Bishop
Congress . . . . General Convention
Senate . . . . House of Bishops
House of Representatives . . . . . House of Deputies

State . . . . Diocese
Governor . . . . Bishop
State Legislature . . . . Diocesan Convention

City . . . . Parish
Mayor . . . . Rector or Vicar
City Council . . . . Vestry

(The largest Protestant denominations in the United States are the Southern Baptist Convention and the Methodist Church.) About half of all Episcopal churches have two hundred or fewer members. A few have members numbering in the thousands.

STRUCTURE OF THE CHURCH: A BIRD'S-EYE VIEW

A helpful way to get a handle on the way the Episcopal Church is governed is to look at its parallels to U.S. government. The box above shows the similarities.

Just as the U.S. government has three levels of government — federal, state, and local — the Episcopal Church is divided into three levels, too — churchwide, diocesan, and parish, each with its own elected leader. The presiding bishop is the leader of the Episcopal Church; bishops lead dioceses; and rectors lead parishes. Just as with U.S. government, each level of the church government has its own law-making body. The Episcopal Church is governed by two houses — the House of Bishops and the House of Deputies. You probably recognize the parallels with the two houses of the U.S. Congress.

YOUR LOCAL CHURCH

So far we know that the universal church is made up of all baptized Christians, but what about the church where you worship, study, pray, and meet friends? Most of the seventy-two hundred churches in the Episcopal Church are **parishes** — self-supporting communities that worship regularly together. A priest who leads the parish is called its **rector**. Rectors are elected by the vestry, the governing body of the parish, and confirmed by the bishop of the diocese.

Members of a Parish

Although all baptized are members of the universal church, the particular parish you belong to depends on Episcopal Church rules. When you were baptized, your name was recorded as a member of that parish. You officially became a *member of record*. If you change parishes, you can transfer your membership by requesting a *letter of transfer* from your original parish.

The **Canons of the General Convention**, the written rules that govern the Episcopal Church, recognize members who are sixteen years and older as adult members. Whether this is sufficient for voting at a particular church depends on that church's by-laws and the laws of the state.

The shield of the Episcopal Church.

Not everyone who attends a church becomes a formal member, and not all formal members attend church regularly. **Communicants** are members who have received communion at least three times in the previous year. A **communicant in good standing** is a communicant who has been "faithful in working, praying, and giving for the spread of the kingdom of God" (Canons of General Convention).

Governance of a Parish

The way a parish is governed depends on the laws of each diocese and state, as well as on the parish's by-laws, the written rules that set out how a parish is governed. Every year, a parish has an annual meeting when members discuss plans for the coming year and share their concerns. At this meeting, members usually vote on the parish budget and elect members of the vestry. They also elect delegates to the diocesan convention.

Because it's difficult for every single member of the church to get together to discuss all the issues of running the parish, they elect a small group, called a **vestry**, to supervise and make decisions about the local church's mission, finances, and buildings and grounds between annual meetings. The size of the vestry, term of office, and requirements for election depend on the by-laws of the parish and in some cases the laws of the state.

The church membership or the vestry elects two officers — a senior warden and a junior warden — either from among the church members or from the vestry. In some parishes, the rector selects the senior warden. Traditionally the senior warden acts as a link between the rector and the parish, while the junior warden supervises the buildings and grounds. The rector presides at vestry meetings, unless he or she asks the senior warden to do so.

Every church has by-laws. These laws, adopted by the members of the parish, determine such things as who is eligible for election to the vestry, how officers are elected, and when the annual meeting is held. The by-laws of a church must be consistent with the canons (rules) of its diocese and the Episcopal Church.

Mission and Ministry

The Catechism in the Book of Common Prayer (page 855) tells us that the mission of the church is "to restore all people to unity with God and each other in Christ." It doesn't say anything about buildings, clergy, vestries, or budgets! But all those ordinary details help the church carry out its primary mission. Vestries oversee budgets, the clergy lead worship, committees carry out the work of Christian education and community service. In the next chapter we carefully explore the ministry of the church. For now, let's continue to look at the way the church organization helps make that ministry happen.

How does your church live into God's strong verbs: repent, be, do, give, forgive, go, sow, pray, judge not, fear not, feed the hungry, clothe the naked, heal the sick, welcome the stranger...?

YOUR DIOCESE

The Episcopal Church isn't a congregational church: it acts not on its own but as part of a **diocese** led by a bishop. A diocese is the basic mission and administrative unit of the Episcopal Church. Individual churches act within the rules of the diocese — and share a common mission.

Your diocese is one of 110 dioceses in the Episcopal Church (100 domestic and 10 international), which range in size from twenty or thirty to almost two hundred churches. The largest domestic diocese is the Diocese of Virginia (one of three in the state of Virginia) with nearly two hundred churches and ninety thousand members. The smallest diocese is the Diocese of Eau Claire (one of three in Wisconsin), with twenty-two churches and fewer than three thousand members. Many dioceses cover entire states. Others, in densely populated states, cover only portions of a state. The state of New York, for example, is made up of six dioceses, while the entire state of Wyoming is one diocese.

Each parish contributes financially to the diocese to pay the salary of the bishop and diocesan staff and to help run diocesan programs, including the Domestic and Foreign Missionary Society of the Episcopal Church. Members of parishes also serve on diocesan committees and participate in and lead diocesan ministries.

Your Bishop

Your bishop is an ordained priest and serves as the chief priest and pastor of the church. In the early church, a bishop (in Greek, *episkopos* means overseer) was an elder appointed by a community of believers. As Christian communities grew, bishops began to lead other parishes close by in addition to their own. The responsibilities of a bishop continue to be to oversee and supervise the churches in the diocese and to serve as pastor to the clergy and their families.

> Bishops represent the connection of all parishes within a diocese, the connection of all dioceses to one another, and the connection of the church today with the early Christian church established by the apostles.

Bishops have authority over matters of faith, discipline, and worship within their diocese. Bishops ordain priests and deacons, ordain other bishops, confirm those who wish to receive the sacrament of confirmation (confirmands), and preside at their diocesan conventions.

In most dioceses, one parish church serves as the diocese's **cathedral**. The word "cathedral" is derived from the Latin word *cathedra*, that is, the teaching seat of the bishop and the oldest sign of the authority of a bishop. It's similar to the county seat of government. A cathedral doesn't have to be a big, fancy church. In fact, the cathedral of the Diocese of Virginia has no walls. It is an outdoor church whose roof is a canopy of trees in the Shenandoah Valley. What makes a church a cathedral is that it houses the bishop's cathedra. A cathedral is the principal church for the diocese and commonly hosts diocesan events and Episcopal services such as ordinations of priests and deacons and the ordination of a bishop. The lead clergyperson at a cathedral is called a **dean**; assisting clergy at a cathedral may be called **canons**.

The Diocesan Convention

Each year the diocese holds a **Diocesan Convention** of both laypeople and clergy. All clergy in a diocese, plus a number of elected lay ministers from each parish, are given seat, voice, and vote at convention. Some dioceses have youth representatives. (The number of laypeople that a parish sends generally depends on the size of the parish.) All representatives to convention, clergy and laity alike, elect officers to various commissions and councils of the diocese and vote on the diocese's mission, ministry, and budget. They may also vote to change the Diocesan Constitution and Canons.

Diocesan Constitution and Canons

Diocesan Constitution and Canons are similar to a parish's by-laws. They're the rules that govern a diocese. These rules determine things like starting new churches, dealing with churches whose membership is dwindling, electing a bishop, sending delegates to convention, choosing committees, making rules governing parish vestries, and deciding on the duties of diocesan officers. The Constitution and Canons are accepted and modified by diocesan convention, but they must always be consistent with the Constitution and Canons of the Episcopal Church.

Diocesan Council

Between conventions, the business of the diocese is coordinated by a **Diocesan Council**. Diocesan councils are similar to vestries in a parish. They act on behalf of the diocesan convention during the year. The diocesan council is usually made up of the bishop and other elected clergy and lay members.

Election of a Bishop

A diocesan convention is called to elect a new bishop. Usually a nominating committee is formed that reviews resumés and interviews candidates. Delegates to convention meet the candidates and vote on a bishop. Election usually requires a majority of both lay and clergy delegates at the special convention. Just as a rector must be approved by the bishop, the election of a bishop must be confirmed by a majority of bishops in the Episcopal Church. A bishop is ordained by three other bishops by the laying on of hands, which expresses our belief that the ministry of bishop is a gift of the Holy Spirit. The three bishops symbolize a continuous apostolic ministry and the communion of all Christian communities with one another.

Some dioceses are so large that one bishop can't serve all churches in the diocese alone, so they elect another bishop to help. The diocese can elect either a *bishop suffragan,* who can't become bishop or, with the consent of the bishop diocesan, a *bishop coadjutor* who succeeds the diocesan bishop. A bishop diocesan can also appoint a *bishop assisting.*

Companion Dioceses

Some dioceses in the Episcopal Church have developed companion relationships with other dioceses throughout the Anglican Communion. Over one hundred companion relationships exist today. Examples are the relationship between the Diocese of Bethlehem in Pennsylvania and Kajo Keji in southern Sudan and between the Diocese of California and the Beijing Christian Council of China. Companion dioceses usually pray for one another weekly, support one another with material and spiritual resources, and initiate joint programming to share their experiences and learn together.

> Companion diocese relationships acknowledge a shared mission by all dioceses throughout the world — to restore all people to unity with God and each other in Christ.

Provinces

Dioceses are clustered geographically into nine provinces. The map on pages 96 and 97 shows all nine provinces of the Episcopal Church. Notice that Province IX is made up of churches in Central and South America. Each province holds leadership conferences twice a year to discuss common issues. Provinces, however, hold no governing authority over their member dioceses.

THE EPISCOPAL CHURCH AT THE CHURCHWIDE LEVEL

Each diocese is part of the Episcopal Church in the United States of America, whose chief pastor is the presiding bishop. Governance within the Episcopal Church rests in the **General Convention**, the legislative body of the Episcopal Church, which meets once every three years to approve programs and budget.

Provinces
of the
Episcopal Church

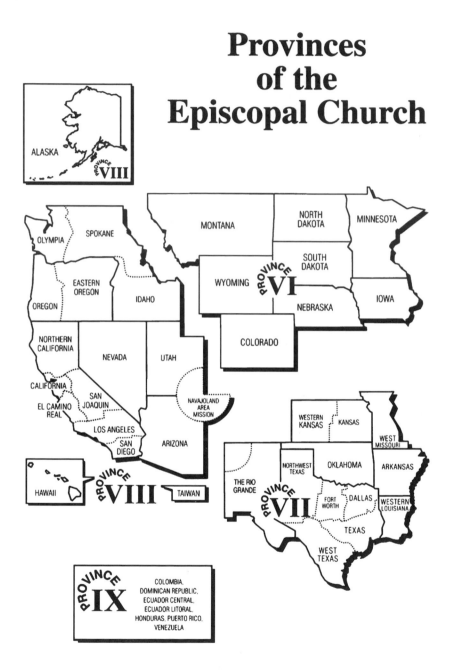

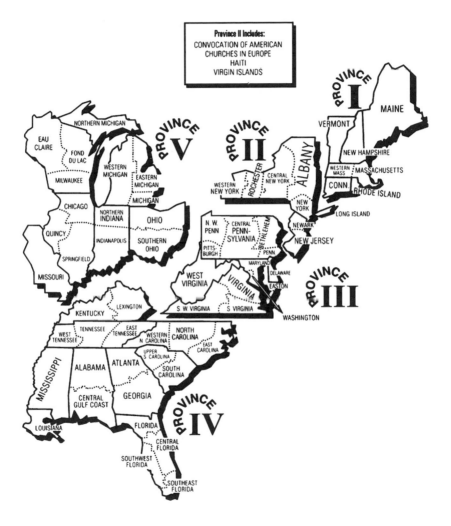

Province II Includes:
CONVOCATION OF AMERICAN
CHURCHES IN EUROPE
HAITI
VIRGIN ISLANDS

PROVINCE I

MAINE
VERMONT
NEW HAMPSHIRE
WESTERN MASS
MASSACHUSETTS
CONN.
RHODE ISLAND

PROVINCE V

NORTHERN MICHIGAN
EAU CLAIRE
FOND DU LAC
WESTERN MICHIGAN
EASTERN MICHIGAN
MILWAUKEE
MICHIGAN
CHICAGO
NORTHERN INDIANA
OHIO
QUINCY
INDIANAPOLIS
SOUTHERN OHIO
SPRINGFIELD
MISSOURI

PROVINCE II

WESTERN NEW YORK
ROCHESTER
CENTRAL NEW YORK
ALBANY
NEW YORK
LONG ISLAND
N. W. PENN
CENTRAL PENN-SYLVANIA
BETHLEHEM
NEWARK
NEW JERSEY
PITTS-BURGH
PENN.
MARYLAND
DELAWARE
EASTON

WEST VIRGINIA
VIRGINIA
WASHINGTON

PROVINCE III

KENTUCKY
LEXINGTON
S. W. VIRGINIA
S VIRGINIA

WEST TENNESSEE
TENNESSEE
EAST TENNESSEE
WESTERN N CAROLINA
NORTH CAROLINA
EAST CAROLINA
UPPER S CAROLINA
MISSISSIPPI
ALABAMA
ATLANTA
SOUTH CAROLINA
CENTRAL GULF COAST
GEORGIA
LOUISIANA
FLORIDA

PROVINCE IV

CENTRAL FLORIDA
SOUTHWEST FLORIDA
SOUTHEAST FLORIDA

Just like the U.S. Congress, General Convention is made up of two legislative bodies — the **House of Bishops** and the **House of Deputies**. The House of Bishops is made up of all bishops — both active and retired. It has about three hundred members. It meets at General Convention to consider legislation and it meets twice a year between conventions for worship, prayer, study, and dialogue. At these between-convention meetings, the House of Bishops often issues pastoral statements that offer guidance and advice to members of the church.

The House of Deputies has about nine hundred members — four clergy and four lay deputies from each diocese. Each province also sends two youth to General Convention. They have seat and voice, but no vote, in the House of Deputies. A president of the House of Deputies is elected from among the deputies. With bishops, deputies, youth, and a multitude of observers, over fifteen thousand people attend General Convention.

The Presiding Bishop

The **presiding bishop** is the Episcopal Church's chief pastor and representative to the world. At one time the senior bishop present at meetings was the presiding bishop; today the presiding bishop is elected by the House of Bishops and confirmed by the House of Deputies and serves for a period of nine years, or until his or her seventieth birthday. The presiding bishop leads the Episcopal Church by serving as its spokesperson to churches throughout the world and providing guidance and vision for the Episcopal Church. As presiding bishop, he or she presides at the House of Bishops and General Convention. He or she visits all dioceses of the church and is often the chief consecrator at the ordination of a bishop. As is true for all members of the Episcopal Church, the presiding bishop must act within the Constitution and Canons of the church.

Not all the heads of churches in the Anglican Communion are elected. For example, the archbishop of Canterbury, the head of the Church of England, is appointed by the prime minister of England.

Executive Council

Between General Conventions, the business of the Episcopal Church is carried out by the **Executive Council**. The Executive Council takes care of "the coordination, development, and implementation of the ministry and mission of the church." That means it carries out the resolutions of the General Convention. The presiding bishop and the president of the House of Deputies are respectively president and vice-president of Executive Council.

Budget

The annual budget for the Episcopal Church when this book went to press was about $55 million, about $25 for every baptized member of the Episcopal Church. Individual churches have a combined budget of $2.2 billion for their mission and ministry, over $1,000 for every member. This reflects that most of the ministry of the church is at the parish and diocesan levels. Through their dioceses, parishes fund about two-thirds of the national church's budget. The rest comes from earnings from investments and government grants.

The budget of the Episcopal Church is divided into canonical, corporate, mission, and ministry expenses. Nearly 60 percent of the budget funds four mission centers of the Episcopal Church — advocacy, mission leadership, evangelism and congregational life, and partnerships. About 12 percent of the budget funds canonical expenses of General Convention and the presiding bishop's office. The remainder funds communication, finance, and general administration. Three-fifths of the budget is funded by *askings* of dioceses for contributions of about 20 percent of diocesan income, and 20 percent comes from investment income; the remainder is from a variety of sources.

The budget is proposed by the Joint Standing Committee on Program, Budget, and Finance and reflects the priorities adopted by the General Convention. The 2007–2009 budget includes five priorities:

1. **Justice and Peace:** Promoting justice and peace for all of God's creation and continuing and accelerating the leadership role and programs of the Episcopal Church, which support the eight Millennium Development Goals in the dioceses of the Episcopal Church and in the world.

2. **Young Adults, Youth, and Children:** Reaching out to young adults, youth, and children through intentional inclusion and full incorporation in the thinking, work, worship, and structure of the church.

3. **Reconciliation and Evangelism:** Reconciling and engaging those who do not know Christ by participating in God's mission of reconciling all things to Christ and proclaiming the Gospel to those who are not yet members of the church.

4. **Congregational Transformation:** Revitalizing and transforming congregations through commitment to leadership development, spiritual

growth, lifelong learning, dynamic and inclusive worship, greater diversity, and mission.

5. **Partnerships:** Reaffirming the importance of our partnerships with provinces of the Anglican Communion and beyond and our relationships with ecumenical and interfaith partners.[10]

 What story is God telling through these five priorities of Episcopal Church?

Constitution and Canons of the Episcopal Church

Although there is a lot of diversity within the Episcopal Church, local churches can't do whatever they please. They live within the Constitution and Canons of the Episcopal Church. There are, for example, specific rules about marriage and remarriage as well as which prayers we can use during services, although these rules aren't set in stone. Delegates can vote to change these rules through resolutions. Those passed by General Convention become **Acts of the General Convention** and govern our life as Episcopalians. *Episcopalarchives.org* publishes all acts of convention.

An Example of Legislation: The Book of Common Prayer

The Book of Common Prayer contains the liturgy, prayers, and instructions for common worship in the Episcopal Church. To be *official*, it must be accepted by General Convention. Every church in the Episcopal Church worships using the Book of Common Prayer; a priest who doesn't follow the instructions within the prayer book can be reprimanded by the bishop. But because our language and culture change continually, along with the way we understand God and the church, from time to time we change and update the prayer book. Reading the opening Prayer of the Eucharist in the prayer book of 1549 shows us the change in language:

> ALMIGHTIE God, unto whom all hartes bee open, and all desyres knowen, and from whom no secretes are hid: clense the thoughtes of our hartes, by the inspiracion of thy holy spirite: that we may perfectly love thee, and worthely magnifie thy holy name: through Christ our Lorde. Amen.[11]
>
> (*Prayer Book* of 1549 as published at *justus.anglican.org*)

---

10. *The Budget of the Episcopal Church, 2007–2009*, 75th General Convention, 2006.
11. *First and Second Prayer-Books of Edward VI* (London: J. M. Dent and Sons, 1910), 212.

To keep our liturgy vibrant, the Book of Common Prayer must change too. Revisions and additions to the prayer book are developed by the Standing Liturgical Commission, a group of clergy and laypersons elected by General Convention that meets both at and between conventions. Let's consider the process that led to the 1979 Book of Common Prayer.

Beginning in 1950, the Standing Liturgical Commission published a series of studies on the 1928 prayer book. In 1967, it proposed a new Rite of Holy Eucharist, which was passed at General Convention for trial use. In 1970, a series of new rites of Holy Eucharist were passed. These new rites were used on a trial basis by a number of parishes throughout the country that gave feedback to the Standing Liturgical Commission. In 1973, additional rites and revisions, which included initiation, the Daily Office, and the Psalter, were authorized and again tried out throughout the church. In 1976, the commission submitted a draft Book of Common Prayer, which was passed as the official prayer book in 1979 under Title II, Canon 3 of the Canons of the Episcopal Church.

At each General Convention, both the House of Bishops and House of Deputies discussed the revisions and additions, and the prayer book became official when it was approved by a majority in both houses. The approval of the prayer book is a good example of the conversations among all members of the church, which is how the Episcopal Church is governed.

ANGLICAN COMMUNION

The Episcopal Church is a member of the **Anglican Communion,** a group of 44 independently governed churches in more than 160 countries that share a common faith, history, and tradition. Member churches of the Anglican Communion, such as the Church of England and the Church of the Province of Southern Africa, are called provinces. Each church has its own chief bishop, known as a **primate,** and its own rules. (The primate of the Episcopal Church is the presiding bishop.) No primate has jurisdiction over the members of another province within the Anglican Communion.

Anglican churches share a common history in the Church of England and express their faith, liturgy, and sacraments in a Book of Common

The compass rose is the official symbol of the Anglican Communion.

Prayer (though not all with the same Book of Common Prayer). Four principles unite churches in the Anglican Communion:

1. The Old and New Testaments are the revealed word of God.

2. The Nicene Creed is our statement of Christian faith.

3. Two sacraments are baptism and Holy Eucharist.

4. Bishops follow a succession of ordination from the apostles to the present.

You can read the exact wording on pages 876–77 in the Book of Common Prayer.

Sharing in these principles, however, does not by itself mean a province is a member of the Anglican Communion. A province is recognized as a member of the Anglican Communion when that province's bishop is invited by the **archbishop of Canterbury** (the primate of the Church of England) to the Lambeth Conference and the membership of the province's bishop is recognized by the Anglican Consultative Council. The Lambeth Conference is a gathering of bishops held every ten years at Lambeth Palace, the official residence of the archbishop of Canterbury.

The archbishop of Canterbury is considered the *first among equals*, emphasizing the equality and joint authority of all primates. He does not have the authority to tell any church in the Anglican Communion what to do.

The archbishop of Canterbury, the Lambeth Conference, the Primates' Meetings, and the Anglican Consultative Council are the "instruments of unity" for the Anglican Communion. See *www.anglicancommunion.org* for more information.

The most basic way Anglican churches express their unity is to meet in dialogue, prayer, fellowship, Bible study, and Eucharist. The Lambeth Conference is one way of doing this. Another is the **Primates' Meetings**, an annual gathering of all primates in the Anglican Communion. A third is the **Anglican Consultative Council**, a gathering of laypeople, bishops, priests, and deacons from churches throughout the Anglican Communion.

By gathering together as one, the Anglican Communion can work together to serve God's mission in the world. The Lambeth Conference, Primates' Meetings, and the Anglican Consultative Council are responsible for activities and projects such as helping to relieve suffering in the world. It also maintains the Office of the Anglican Observer to the UN to express its concerns and collect and share information about UN initiatives.

The Anglican Communion, as you can see, has a loose definition. Who belongs is who attends its meetings. In the early 2000s the "bonds of affection" (sense of unity) were strained when the Episcopal Church confirmed the election of an openly gay priest as bishop of New Hampshire and the Anglican Church of Canada adopted liturgies to bless same-sex unions. In response to these events, a commission of the Anglican Communion proposed a covenant that more specifically defined what it means to be in communion. And at a Primates Meeting in 2005, the Episcopal Church and the Anglican Church of Canada were requested to withdraw their delegates from the Anglican Consultative Council. The two churches withdrew from official participation, but continued to send observers. The primates continue in respectful dialogue, balancing what it means to be of one mind against the strength that one voice can provide to address worldwide issues regarding human rights and poverty.

GOD'S PROMISE TO THE NEW CHURCH

After the Holy Spirit descended upon the apostles, Peter spoke, recalling the words of the prophet Joel:

> *In the last days it will be, God declares*
> *that I will pour out my Spirit upon all flesh*
> *and your sons and your daughters shall prophesy,*
> *and your young men shall see visions,*
> *and your old men shall dream dreams.* (Acts 2:17)

What can we learn from this sermon? After receiving the Holy Spirit, we are called to "prophesy" and "see visions." We are invited to become part of God's dream. We are the active hands of Christ in the world who can work with God to bring God's kingdom near. We are charged to do the work of the church. The structure of the church is a mechanism to do that good work. Some ways you can become involved in the structure of the church are:

+ Attend the annual meeting at your parish.

+ Consider serving on the vestry. The vestry helps define how the ministry of the church is applied in your community.

- Attend diocesan conventions and consider running for delegate to convention.

- Subscribe to your diocesan newspaper in print or online to become informed of the mission and ministry of your diocese.

Dream dreams and prophesy your vision to the church. The governing bodies of the church set the policy and rules of the church so important to its ministry.

✝ TRANSFORMING QUESTIONS

1. **Be Attentive:** Look at the five priorities of the Episcopal Church during the 2007-9 triennium. (You can find the list on page 99.) Recall an instance of when you did something that fulfills one of those priorities. What do you remember?

2. **Be Intelligent:** What does your experience mean for you? What other meanings are possible?

3. **Be Reasonable:** What story from the Bible, hymn, or liturgy relates to your experience? Read it. How does it challenge or confirm your understanding? Does your understanding provide new insights?

4. **Be Responsible:** What will you do as a result of your understanding?

5. **Be in Love Transformed:** Research the new priorities of the next triennium (2009 and 2012). (Look on *episcopalchurch.org*.) What does your experience explored here and the new priorities suggest that you do differently?

Chapter Seven

What Is God Calling You to Do?

DO

During one of your readings through the four Gospels, circle or underline the strong verbs of God's good news. Repent. Be. Do. Give. Forgive. Feed. Clothe. Go. Sow. Pray. Heal. Judge not. Fear not. Cast out. Trust.

You will find that many of those strong verbs introduce Gospel imperatives. Marching orders. Mission statements.

Feed the hungry. Clothe the naked. Heal the sick. Welcome the stranger. Visit the imprisoned. Raise the dead. Proclaim good news. Sell what you have and give the money to the poor. Love God with all your heart. Love your neighbor as yourself. Love your enemies. Pray for those who persecute you. Be reconciled. Take up your cross. Follow me. Lose your life for my sake and you will find it. Make disciples.

An impossible job description begins to be written on our hearts when we promise, or renew our promises, to "believe in God the Father...in Jesus Christ, the Son of God...in God the Holy Spirit [and] to continue in the apostles' teaching and fellowship, in the breaking of bread, and in the prayers...to persevere in resisting evil, and whenever you fall into sin, repent and return to the Lord...to proclaim by word and example the Good News of God in Christ...to seek and serve Christ in all persons, loving your neighbor as yourself...to strive for justice and peace among all people, and respect the dignity of every human being" (Book of Common Prayer, pages 92–94).

"The Baptismal Covenant," according to Bethlehem Diocese Bishop Paul Marshall, "contains perhaps the strongest statement the Episcopal Church has ever put forward concerning the obligations Christians take on in terms of faith and life....It combines faith in God with active discipleship that respects the dignity and freedom of every human being."

"I will, with God's help," we say, each time we renew those baptismal promises.

"Jesus of Nazareth is a troubling and troublesome figure," Verna Dozier wrote in *The Dream of God,* "and the church has never known what to do with him." This is why your best way into or through the Episcopal Church is to read and inwardly digest the sacred scriptures. Not as individual verses, but each book in the context of all the other books, the tradition of the church, your experience of God's love and your love for your sisters and brothers, and your critical thinking and reasoning about all of this.

Jesus challenges us to dream. The Holy Spirit draws God's dream from deep within us. To pray is to dream, to hope, to expect, to imagine. Whether worshiping with a community, reading alone, reflecting on the Bible, considering a personal experience, a story, or a movie, we can be at prayer.

"Only the contemplative," Thomas Merton used to say, only the pray-er "knows what the scoop is." Only the pray-er knows that the really real is God breaking into human history so we might break out with new God-given hearts to pursue God's reality, God's heart's desires.

Don't let others tell you what is real. Imagine God's reality. See things differently. Magnify the Lord. See God large in your life. Allow God within you to transform you and the world through you.   *— B.L.*

◆ ◆ ◆

The "strong verbs of God's good news" that Bill reminds us are gospel imperatives — feed, clothe, heal, welcome, visit, raise, proclaim — are verbs of servant ministry. The call to servanthood is found throughout the Bible. We begin by looking at ministry with the "Servant Song" from Isaiah:

> *Here is my servant, whom I uphold,*
>   *my chosen, in whom my soul delights;*
> *I have put my spirit upon him;*
>   *he will bring forth justice to the nations.*
> *He will not cry or lift up his voice,*
>   *or make it heard in the street;*
> *A bruised reed he will not break,*
>   *and a dimly burning wick he will not quench;*
> *he will faithfully bring forth justice.*
>
> (Isaiah 42:1–3)

Read the passage above slowly to yourself. Pause. Read it again. After the second reading, ask yourself, "Who is the servant?" "What is the servant being called to do?" This Servant Song was written as a call to Israel. God calls his chosen people, Israel, to a particular mission — a mission of justice. We see this song again in the New Testament, but this time for God's servant Jesus:

> *Here is my servant, whom I have chosen,*
>   *my beloved, with whom my soul is well pleased.*
> *I will put my Spirit upon him,*
>   *and he will proclaim justice to the Gentiles.*

> *He will not wrangle or cry aloud,*
> *nor will anyone hear his voice in the streets.*
> *He will not break a bruised reed*
> *or quench a smoldering wick*
> *until he brings justice to victory.*
> *And in this name the Gentiles will hope.*
> (Matthew 12:18–21)

The first sentence echoes the voice of God at Jesus' baptism — "This is my Son, the Beloved, with whom I am well pleased." God claims his son as chosen and loved. The second sentence declares that the Holy Spirit has descended on Jesus, giving him the gifts to fulfill his mission — the same mission God gave to Israel to proclaim justice.

We've received that mission too. As baptized members of the body of Christ, we inherit the role of servant. We're chosen by God and helped by the Holy Spirit to bring justice to our communities. Through our baptism we become Christ-bearers, promising to take up Christ's mission, the reign of God. Israel's Servant Song is our Servant Song.

Return to the Servant Song on page 106 of this chapter and read it one more time. Cross out each "he" and "him" and insert your own name. Read it again and imagine yourself as the servant of God who upholds you and whose Spirit rests on you. How does that feel? What are you called to do as a servant of God?

Be attentive to what you have read from Isaiah and Matthew — and to matters of the heart. Be intelligent. How do you understand what you have heard? Be reasonable. What is the best way in your life situation to understand what you have heard? Be responsible about what you intend to do as a result of how you understand what you have heard. Be in Love as you do it.

BAPTISMAL PROMISES

At baptism each of us made five promises, called **baptismal promises**, or someone made them for us. These are promises to do the work God has given us to do in the world — our mission. Whenever we witness a baptism, confirmation, or reaffirmation we renew our promises by answering, "I will, with God's help":

Will you continue in the apostles' teaching and fellowship, in the breaking of the bread, and in the prayers? *I will, with God's help.*

Will you persevere in resisting evil, and whenever you fall into sin, repent, and return to the Lord? *I will, with God's help.*

Will you proclaim by word and example the good news of God in Christ? *I will, with God's help.*

Will you seek and serve Christ in all persons, loving your neighbor as yourself? *I will, with God's help.*

Will you strive for justice and peace among all people, and respect the dignity of every human being? *I will, with God's help.*

Our promises begin with the community — the community of Christ's body, the church — which nourishes us and encourages us to keep our baptismal promises. This first promise reminds us that we know ourselves first as members of a community of faith and that praying and receiving the sacraments prepares us for our work in the world. The second promise reminds us that before going out into the world we must make things right with ourselves — we must live according to God's will. We promise to resist evil and when we sin, to turn away and return to God.

We get our moral authority, as Christians, as Episcopalians, from our baptismal vows.... These promises we make are a bit like the chicken egg swallowed by the snake. It is in there, but it takes a while to digest.   —Bonnie Anderson[12]

The final three promises tell us about our work in the world — how we are to be servants to others. We are to share the good news of God's love to all people with both our words and how we behave. That is, our actions are to reflect God's love. We are to seek and serve Christ in all people. That is, to look for the goodness in others and treat others as if they are Christ himself. As Matthew's Gospel says in the parable of the goats and sheep, "Truly I tell you, just as you did it to one of the least of these who are members of my family, you did it to me." We do this by feeding the hungry, clothing the poor, providing shelter for the homeless, and caring for the sick. In all that we do, we promise to strive for justice and peace among all people, that is, to deal fairly and honestly with others and work toward bringing all people

---

12. Sermon by Bonnie Anderson, president, House of Deputies, Grace Cathedral, San Francisco, October 19, 2008.

together as one community. Because we are baptized Christians, living out these promises is our ministry.

MINISTERS: WHO WE ARE

In the last chapter you read a little about **ministry** — our ways of serving others. The Episcopal Church recognizes all baptized people as ministers of God's kingdom. The ministers are laypersons, bishops, priests, and deacons. Everyone who's been baptized shares a common ministry: representing Christ and his church. Laypeople also have another ministry:

> to bear witness to him wherever they may be; and, according to the gifts given them, to carry on Christ's work of reconciliation in the world; and to take their place in the life, worship, and governance of the Church. (Book of Common Prayer, page 855)

You are a minister. And your ministry right now is as a layperson. Ninety-nine percent of God's people are called to this important lay ministry. Read the description again and notice how it matches our baptismal promises that related to our work in the world.

- We're called "to bear witness to him." This is the third promise we make at baptism.

- We're called to "carry on Christ's work of reconciliation in the world." This fulfills our fourth and fifth promises.

Let's look at this second part a little more closely. What does reconciliation mean? Have you ever reconciled a bank statement? You compare your written record of deposits and withdrawals with the bank's records and make adjustments to your account until the two match. Think about the reconciliation of the world the same way. There are two things: the world as we actually live it and the world as God calls us to live (God's kingdom). So the work of reconciliation is making adjustments in how we live in an effort to make those two worlds match.

Anointed into a Royal Priesthood

You might still feel a little uncomfortable thinking of yourself as a minister. What makes us ministers in God's kingdom is our baptism. Just as Jesus was anointed by the Holy Spirit when he was baptized, so were we. And after we were baptized we were anointed with oil of chrism, blessed so that everyone sealed with it shares in the royal priesthood of Jesus Christ. In the New

Testament book of 1 Peter, the writer tells early Christians the very same thing: "You are a chosen race, a royal priesthood, a holy nation."

The oil you were sealed with has a long history that symbolizes our priesthood and our ministry. Samuel poured an entire horn filled with oil on David's head to anoint him king of Israel (1 Samuel 16:13). God anointed prophets (Isaiah 61:1). A woman with an alabaster jar anointed Jesus with expensive oil before his death and resurrection (Matthew 26:7). We were anointed into our ministry with the oil of kings and prophets.

Our Ministry Proclaims God's Dream for Creation

So how do we live our ministry today? Many of us have loving families and friends, times when we laugh with others, basically healthy minds and bodies, and not too many roadblocks getting in the way of what we want. Some of us may face difficulties — loneliness, grief for the loss of a loved one, sickness and disease, and perhaps days we don't have enough to eat or warm clothes to wear. The world falls short of what God would like. Although we may see signs of God's kingdom — like when we experience joy — it isn't here completely. To know what our ministry is, we need to understand what that kingdom looks like and figure out what we can do to make it happen. So the first step is to figure out what the kingdom of God is.[13]

✠   "God says to you, 'I have a dream. Please help me to realize it. It is a dream of a world whose ugliness and squalor and poverty, its war and hostility, its greed and harsh competitiveness, its alienation and disharmony are changed into their glorious counterparts'" (Desmond Tutu).[14] What dream does God tell you?

GOD'S DREAM IN THE JEWISH SCRIPTURES

God is always telling us what his kingdom is all about. It's a world filled with joy, a world of relationships with others, a world where our needs are met,

---

13. I am indebted to John L. Kater Jr. and his unpublished work, "The Persistence of the Gospel," for guiding much of the discussion of the reign of God.

14. Desmond Tutu and Douglas Abrams, *God Has a Dream: A Vision of Hope for Our Time* (New York: Doubleday, 2004), 19.

and a world where people are honest and fair. At the beginning, God created plants and creatures of every kind, of the land, air, and sea — and then blessed them. God created humans and blessed them too. This tells us that God's kingdom is filled with life and joy. God saw that humans were lonely, and provided them with companions. This reminds us that God's kingdom is filled with relationships and community. To each of the creatures he made — the plants, the animals, and the humans — God commanded, "Be fruitful and multiply." God's kingdom is a world where there is enough for everyone. It's a world of abundance. And finally, God gave humans command over every living thing — not for power, but for servanthood. God's kingdom is a world of order and service and a world of justice.

The Bible also has stories about when the world was far from being joyful, abundant, and just. During these times God reminded his people about his kingdom and what he wanted for them. One such time was when the nation of Israel lived in exile in Babylon. They lived as slaves, suffered disease, and didn't live long. But in the midst of this hardship, God sent a prophet to remind them of his kingdom:

> I will rejoice in Jerusalem
> and delight in my people;
> no more shall the sound of weeping be heard in it,
> or the cry of distress.
> No more shall there be in it
> an infant that lives but a few days,
> or an old person who does not live out a lifetime;
> for one who dies at a hundred years will be considered a youth,
> and one who falls short of a hundred will be considered accursed.
> They shall build houses and inhabit them;
> they shall plant vineyards and eat their fruit.
> They shall not build and another inhabit;
> they shall not plant and another eat;
> for like the days of a tree shall the days of my people be,
> and my chosen shall long enjoy the work of their hands.
> They shall not labor in vain,
> or bear children for calamity;
> for they shall be offspring blessed by the LORD —
> and their descendants as well.
> Before they call I will answer,
> while they are yet speaking I will hear.

The wolf and the lamb shall feed together,
    the lion shall eat straw like the ox;
       but the serpent — its food shall be dust!
They shall not hurt or destroy
    on all my holy mountain, says the LORD.
                                    (Isaiah 65:19–25)

This song tells us more about what God's dream for the world looks like. People live long lives, so long that those who live to be a hundred will be youthful. People live in the houses they build and eat the fruit they plant. All people are treated fairly. People do not live without because God provides. God's vision of creation is marked by abundance. They live in community without enemies — where the wolf and lamb feed together. God longs for a community of peace.

JESUS' MINISTRY PROCLAIMING THE KINGDOM OF GOD

Jesus also tells us about what God wishes for creation. The four Gospels tell the story of Jesus proclaiming the coming of the kingdom of God. In Mark, for example, Jesus proclaims, "The time is fulfilled, and the kingdom of God has come near" (Mark 1:15). Jesus spoke about God's dreams as the kingdom of God, a place where God's will rules. Jesus used the word "kingdom" because people were ruled by kings and were familiar with kingdoms.

Jesus' words and actions showed us God's dream for us by bringing joy, community, abundance, and justice to the world. One of the first things Jesus did after his baptism was to call together a community of people — his disciples. They worshiped, studied, and prayed together, and they saw Jesus performing miracles, healing, forgiving, and gathering more people together. Jesus also sent this group of ordinary people to continue to do God's work in the world.

If these seemingly unworthy followers of Jesus could help bring about God's kingdom, we can too.

The people Jesus called were ordinary people just like us. Some were fishermen; others did work that was despised in the Jewish community, like collecting taxes. They weren't the smartest or the most faithful. Lots of times they doubted Jesus, and they fought over who was the most important. They weren't reliable either. After all, they fell asleep in the garden the night before Jesus was crucified, even though he asked them to stay up with him. They had weaknesses just like we do. All this tells us that we too can be part of

God's community. God's kingdom is a place where we live with one another in community.

Justice

Soon after calling the first disciples Jesus told them about the kingdom of God in the Sermon on the Mount, or the Beatitudes: Blessed are those who mourn, blessed are the meek, blessed are those who hunger, blessed are the merciful, blessed are the pure in heart, blessed are the peacemakers, blessed are the persecuted, and the reviled (Matthew 5). They are blessed because they will be comforted, inherit the earth, be filled, receive mercy, see God, and be called children of God. God's kingdom will be filled with justice.

Life of Joy

Throughout Jesus' ministry he healed the sick and forgave those who had done wrong. Jesus brought them joy. What is amazing in these stories is how important touch was to his ministry of healing and forgiveness. For example, Mark tells us that he touched a leper and said, "Be made clean!" and the leper was cured. A woman who had been hemorrhaging for twelve years touched Jesus' cloak and was healed. Jesus laid his hands on the blind man to restore his sight. Touched by Jesus' healing power, these people could live out their lives with joy free of disease. What we can learn from this is that while we might not be able to heal like Jesus, we can bring others joy by reaching out to them to let them know we care. And we can offer an embrace or handshake of forgiveness to those who have hurt us. By our touch we can bring joy to the world.

Abundance

Jesus' ministry demonstrated what life is with abundance. When the disciples are faced with a hungry crowd of more than five thousand people and only a few fish and a couple of loaves of bread, Jesus feeds them all — with twelve baskets of food to spare. Nothing runs out. When people ask him to describe the kingdom of God, Jesus tells about a mustard seed that grows into a tree that provides a home for the birds and yeast mixed with flour that expands into nourishing bread. In Jesus' life of abundance, out of little comes much. We too can share what little we have, and together with others who have little, provide enough for everyone.

Community

Community was central to Jesus' ministry — from calling the disciples to welcoming the outcast to forgiving the sinner. Consider the story of Jesus and Zacchaeus, a tax collector, in Luke 19. As a tax collector for the Roman Empire, Zacchaeus was considered unclean and a sinner. When Jesus came to him, he announced that they would dine together at Zacchaeus's house. So even before Zacchaeus confessed his sins, Jesus forgave him and invited him into his group of friends. Zacchaeus responded by repenting and giving back what he'd stolen. By bringing these outcasts back into the community by forgiving them he gave them the strength to change their lives. Jesus' acts of forgiveness restored community and brought peace. For Jesus, there's always more room at the table, and the community can always be expanded. In the parable of the good Samaritan Jesus tells us that our neighbors are those who society says are unclean. We, like Jesus, can invite others to our community — especially those who don't seem to belong.

WE, TOO, ARE CALLED TO PROCLAIM

Jesus shared this ministry with his disciples, granting them the power and authority to heal and proclaim the kingdom of God. They continued this ministry after Jesus' death and resurrection, and with the power of the Holy Spirit they baptized believers to do the same. Through our baptism we too are part of the community that has been sent out to do God's work. We too are called to a ministry of supporting relationships within community. We too are called to a ministry of abundance by providing for the needs of others. We too are called to a ministry of joy by healing the sick and comforting those who are mourning. We too are called to a ministry of justice by treating others fairly and honestly and asking others to do the same.

> The Baptismal Covenant contains perhaps the strongest statement the Episcopal Church has ever put forward concerning the obligations Christians take on in terms of faith and life.   —Paul Marshall[15]

It's no mistake that our baptismal promises proclaim the kingdom of God. We promise to seek and serve Christ in all persons, loving our neighbor as ourselves. And we promise to strive for justice and peace among all people and respect the dignity of every human being. We are called to do this, as Jesus did, from our community of faith. Through baptism we share in the ministry of Christ, a hands-on ministry marked by healing, forgiveness, blessing,

---

15. Paul V. Marshall, "Answers to Questions to Bishop Candidates for the Diocese of Bethlehem," unpublished, 1995.

and supporting others that proclaims that God's kingdom is near. Through our ministry we participate in God's kingdom of a life of joy, community, abundance, and justice.

WHERE IS OUR MINISTRY?

Ministry happens wherever we are, not just in church. The mission and ministry of the people of God is out in the world. Just as Jesus sent the disciples out into the world to spread the good news, so we too are sent out to serve God throughout the week. Your ministry, then, happens at work, at home with your family, out with friends, and with your neighbors. Where you see people calling together community, living a life of joy, giving generously, and acting justly, you're seeing God's kingdom being proclaimed.

As a community of faith, we gather each week to worship God and to study, pray, and serve together. Just as Jesus maintained a core community, we too must help to nourish our central faith community. We do this in many ways. We take part in our community's worship life as choir members, altar guild members, lectors, or chalice bearers. Or we can lead prayer and study as a Sunday school teacher, a member of a prayer group or a support group. We help at soup kitchens, tutoring programs, homeless shelters, or prisons. By continuing in worship, prayer, study, and service, we're strengthened to go out in the world in peace to love and serve God.

YOU HAVE BEEN GIVEN SPECIAL GIFTS

In letters to early Christian communities in Corinth, Galatia, and Rome, the apostle Paul wrote about **gifts of the Spirit**: talents and abilities God gives us to fulfill our ministry. Paul was addressing the struggles these communities were facing. What were their ministries? What gifts did the people have to fulfill those ministries? How could the individuals in the community work together as one? We continue to ask ourselves these very same questions. This is what we learn from Paul.

There Are a Variety of Gifts

There are a variety of gifts. In 1 Corinthians 12:4–10, Paul lists the following gifts: wisdom, knowledge, faith, healing, working of miracles, prophecy, discernment of spirits, tongues, and the interpretation of tongues. And in Paul's letter to the Romans he lists more gifts: ministry, teaching, exhortation, generosity, diligence, and cheerfulness (Romans 12:6–8). Both lists addressed the needs of the communities to whom Paul had written; neither was meant

Your Ministry

What does your ministry look like? We minister in a variety of ways. Some care for others as healthcare givers, some bring joy to life through music and art, some prepare others for a life of service as teachers, and still others.... To consider how you minister, begin by remembering ways that you fulfill each of your five baptismal promises and write about them below:

I continue in the apostles' teaching and fellowship, in the breaking of the bread, and in the prayers by _____
_____ .

One time that I persevered in resisting evil was when I _____
_____ .

The last time I proclaimed by word and example the good news of God in Christ was when I _____
_____ .

This week I served Christ in a particular person, loving him or her as I love myself, when I _____
_____ .

One action I took that brought justice and peace to my community, and therefore the world, was when I _____
_____ .

Looking at the actions we have already taken to fulfill our baptismal promises gives us some idea of what our ministry is in the world. The answers each one of us has written above are going to differ because each of us is uniquely and wonderfully made. Each of us has received unique gifts to fulfill our ministry.

to be exhaustive. The Spirit gives different gifts at different times to address the changing needs of the community.

You Have at Least One Gift

The Spirit gives at least one gift to every person. And each person's gift is different. How neat is that — to know that God looked at you and gave you your very own gift? God has entrusted you with something valuable.

Nobody Has All the Gifts

Remember, community is important to God. So you shouldn't be surprised to know that, while everyone has at least one gift, you don't, nor does anyone, have them all. You are meant to use your gifts in community. In 1 Corinthians 12 Paul talks about a community as a human body. The body has many parts, each necessary to the health of the body but none sufficient on its own. "If the foot would say, 'Because I am not a hand, I do not belong to the body,' that would not make it any less a part of the body." And also, "The eye cannot say to the hand, 'I have no need of you'" (1 Corinthians 12:15, 21). Suppose the person with vision didn't share her gift. Imagine the harm a body could do if it couldn't see what it was doing! You need to use your gifts along with the gifts of others to serve God's kingdom.

The seven doves represent the seven gifts of the Holy Spirit (see Isa. 11:2; Rev. 5:12).

God Gives Generously

God provides spiritual gifts generously. You, together with others in your community, have all the gifts you need to do what you need to bring about God's kingdom. In fact, God gives even more than we need. Think about the parable of the Sower in Mark's Gospel (4:3–9). The farmer threw seeds all over the place: on the path, on rocky ground, among thorns, and on good soil. God is like that — giving generously and hoping that the seeds will take root. Our job is to receive God's gifts and nurture them to bear fruit.

The 2004 movie *The Incredibles* shows what's possible with abundant gifts. Elastigirl, the mother and caregiver of all, needs to be able to stretch herself in all sorts of directions. And she does. She has the gift of literally stretching herself thin! Violet, the teenager who wants to blend in and protect herself from outsiders, is given her gift in such quantity that she can disappear and generate a protective force field. Dash and Mr. Incredible have oversized gifts too — overconfident Dash can run at superspeeds and Mr. Incredible is superstrong. Take a minute and imagine what you could do if your gifts were supersized. Imagine that you had unlimited generosity or wisdom. What would you do differently?

Use Your Gifts for the Good of Everyone

The Incredibles also illustrates the possibilities when we use our gifts for the good of everyone. This family works together when trouble comes. Elastigirl stretches into a parachute to save her family from falling. Violet protects herself and her brother with her gift of a force field. As Mr. Incredible says, "Having superpowers is great. Having the love of family is truly powerful." We are to use our gifts not to boost ourselves, but to serve others. The apostle Paul tells us the same thing. Each member uses his or her gifts for the good of the family, bringing the community to its greatest ability to live into their call.

An important step in using your gifts for ministry is to claim them and be confident that, indeed, you have enough. What might your gifts be?

You may not be a superhero fit for the big screen, but when you use your gifts in everyday acts of ministry you're an everyday hero. What may seem like simple acts to you can be great acts of ministry to others. Think about saying a simple "hello" and "how are you?" to the cashier at check-out. That simple "hello" might just change that person's whole outlook on their ministry on the job.

You Bring Joy to the World When You Use Your Gifts

God created you and blessed you and wants you, and all of his people, to have joy. So using your gifts will also make you feel good. The apostle Paul talked about joy in terms of the fruit of the Spirit. In his letter to the Galatians (5:22–23) he lists the following fruit: love, joy, peace, patience, kindness, generosity, faithfulness, gentleness, and self-control. The qualities suggest a life of joy in relationship with others.

We are adept at doing many things. Modern life seems to require this! In your daily life, managing your household, fulfilling your work and community obligations, you may be required to write reports, lead meetings, plan events, diagnose diseases, operate heavy machinery, and so on. You are likely good at many things. But just because you might be good at something doesn't mean it is your gift. What makes an ability a gift is that you look forward to using gifts; using your skills tends to deplete your energy. This doesn't mean you cannot or should not use your skills; it is just a way to look for those things that come from your heart — your gifts.

You can use your gifts for lots of purposes. You can use them to bring people together or use them selfishly for your own gain; you can use them to build relationships or to tear them down, to nourish life or to destroy it. What we learn from the Bible and the Christian community is that God has given you gifts to build community, strengthen relationships, nourish and support life, and bring people closer to God. As Christians we recognize that our gifts originate with God and we use them for God's purpose — the kingdom of God — not for our own purposes.

FINDING OUR SPIRITUAL GIFTS

So each of us has gifts for ministry. And each of us has the responsibility to find out what those gifts are. Once we come to know those gifts we can nurture and honor them by offering them to God. We offer them to God by practicing them in our ministry to proclaim the kingdom of God.

The process that helps us come to know our gifts is called discernment. The process of **discernment** pulls apart the various possibilities to allow us to see each more clearly. It is a process of distinguishing the variety of gifts, distinguishing our gifts from those of others, and distinguishing those of the Spirit from gifts not of the Spirit.

> Two questions to ask when discerning your gifts are:
> (1) What do I long to do? and (2) How do the things I long to do fit into God's dreams?

The work of discernment is never finished. Our gifts change, the needs of the community change, and consequently our call will change. These are two very broad questions that you can continue to ask yourself from time to time. You might want to try a more structured exercise of discernment. Here are three exercises that will help you identify specific gifts grounded in scripture and God's work in your life. Try each and see which one most clearly helps you find out who you are and discover what God is calling you to do.

#1 Listing Gifts

Paul listed a number of gifts of the Spirit, which provide a good beginning place. But because communities and cultures change, those gifts will also change. So to add to and update his list, write the four characteristics of the kingdom of God: life of joy, abundance, community, and justice. What abilities do you think would help someone create a world where there is less sorrow and sickness (filled with joy); one where people are no longer hungry, homeless, or in need (is abundant); one where people relate to one another with care (has community); and one that treats people fairly and honestly (has justice)? Write those gifts below each quality that defines God's kingdom. Write as many as you can. Share your list with someone else. Examples are:

Life of joy

Can play an instrument
Laughs and is cheerful
Comforts and/or cures the sick

Community

Forgives
Shows compassion and mercy
Oversees projects
Has a strong faith
Likes to invite

Abundance

Gives generously
Forgives
Shares faith
Has a strong faith

Justice

Knows right from wrong
Can persuade others of what's right
Encourages others
Teaches truth
Counsels others

Gifts likely address more than one aspect of the kingdom of God. Your list provides you with gifts that are actively used today.

#2 People We Admire[16]

Continue with the following exercise to see which of these gifts are also likely to be your gifts. Think about the people you admire and whose actions bring about a world of life in joy, community, abundance, and justice. They can be people you know personally or someone you have read about. They can be contemporary, historical — or even fictional characters from a book or a movie.

List as many of these people as you can. When you're done, underline six who especially stand out for you. Next to each name write three or four

---

16. This exercise is based on one in Lloyd Edwards, *Discerning Your Spiritual Gifts* (Cambridge, Mass.: Cowley Publications, 1988), 55.

things that you admire about this person. For example, suppose you wrote the name of a co-worker who supports your work and with whom you can discuss new ideas. So next to that name, you might write, "encouraging," "wise," and "well-spoken." If you wrote the name of a great leader such as Mahatma Gandhi, you might write "compassionate," "dedicated to peace," and "perseverant" next to his name. Do this for each person you wrote down. When you've finished, look at the qualities you've named. What are the common characteristics you find among those you admire? While the people may live or have lived very different lives from one another, you will likely find similarities in their characters.

What this exercise reveals are the gifts that you value and have yourself. If you do this exercise in a group, you will find that no two people will have the same list. The people whom you name might be similar, but the characteristics that are common to your list are unique to you.

#3 Considering Your Own Life

Already in this chapter you listed examples of how you have acted to fulfill your baptismal promises. Whether you realize it or not, you're already using your gifts. In an exercise of discernment you reflect on your actions to recognize the gifts you are already using. So return to your answers to how you're fulfilling your promises on page 116. Next to each write the talent you used to fulfill that promise. If you wrote a letter to a congressperson about a homeless shelter in your town as an example of bringing justice to the world, you might write "wisdom" and "compassion." Be specific in your answers. How, for example, did wisdom and compassion guide you? You might say "knowledge of local housing ordinances and my knowledge from the Bible of what Jesus asked of his community." And you might add "sense of responsibility for the poor." You see opportunities for ministry differently than everyone else does. Remember, no one has all the gifts—and our gifts complement one another.

> Before you tell your life what you intend to do with it,
> listen for what it intends to do with you.
> —Parker J. Palmer[17]

You now have three lists: one that shows the possibilities, a shorter list of those gifts you see in yourself, and another list of those gifts you've already realized you have. Keep all these gifts in mind as you continue in your ministry, and see how they guide you to respond to the world.

17. Parker J. Palmer, *Let Your Life Speak* (San Francisco: Jossey-Bass, 2000), 3.

The Importance of Community

It's always important to discern our gifts within a community. We do this for many reasons. Discernment is difficult. Our community can give us guidance and perspective. Because we're human, we can be led astray by our own egos and lose sight of God's call to us. Abba Moses, a fifth-century monk living in the deserts of Egypt, told this unfortunate story of another monk, Hero. Hero believed he could discern God's call without the help of his community and so he went to live alone. After a time, Hero came to believe that God, wanting to test his faithfulness, called him to jump into a deep well. Hero jumped in. A few days later, the brothers found Hero and pulled him out. Hero died two days later. Now, this is a dramatic story of someone hearing and acting on voices other than that of God. But we too can be led astray by our own desire to prove ourselves. Our community's guidance doesn't just keep us from going astray; it also shows us gifts we might not recognize ourselves. God wants us to use our gifts in a community that has discerned God's will, and God will give us the gifts we need to do that. But we can't do it by ourselves.

Ignatian Examen

Two very basic questions you can continue to ask yourself each day as a practice of ongoing discernment are:

When did I feel most alive today?

When did I most feel life draining out of me?

These two questions come from the practice of the **Ignatian Examen**, a process individuals can use to find God's call to them. It was developed by a Spanish saint named Ignatius Loyola in the early 1500s. The examen helps people understand God's desires and will for them within their daily lives. The examen is based on the belief that God actively guides us. God speaks to us both in the good and the bad times. The questions might not appear to relate to God directly. By asking God to guide us as we ask ourselves the questions and seek the answers, our reflections and answers are more likely to reflect what God wants of us. There are other sets of questions to use in the practice of examen:

For what moment today am I most grateful?

For what moment today am I least grateful?

and

When was I happiest today?

When was I saddest?[18]

The examen is meant to be practiced regularly. By asking ourselves these questions each day, we will begin to see patterns in our choices and experiences. These patterns suggest our gifts and God's call to us. As you may guess, the times we are happiest, energized, and most grateful are likely to be times when we are using the gifts that God gave us. By asking simple questions we can be open to God's continual call to us to be ministers, bringing our world closer to God's dream for it.

THE IMPORTANCE OF CHURCH TO MINISTRY

When you were baptized, you became a member of the body of Christ — the church — and an inheritor of the kingdom of God. Each week we gather from our various ministries out in the world to thank God for creation and blessings. We offer our prayers for ourselves and others and confess our shortcomings. We ask for God's mercy and forgiveness to help us return our lives to God's way. And we're nourished by the communion bread and wine. We end our worship together each Sunday by asking for the strength to return to the world to do God's will:

> *Eternal God, heavenly Father,*
> *you have graciously accepted us as living members*
> *of your Son our Savior Jesus Christ,*
> *and you have fed us with spiritual food*
> *in the Sacrament of his Body and Blood.*
> *Send us now into the world in peace,*
> *and grant us strength and courage*
> *to love and serve you*
> *with gladness and singleness of heart;*
> *through Christ our Lord. Amen.*
>   (Book of Common Prayer, page 365)

---

18. These questions are from Dennis Linn, Sheila Fabricant Linn, and Matthew Linn, *Sleeping with Bread: Holding What Gives You Life* (Mahwah, N.J.: Paulist, 1995).

✠ TRANSFORMING QUESTIONS

1. **Be Attentive:** Think of a time when you ministered to the needs of a person or group of people. Describe what happened. Where were you? What did you see, hear, taste, smell, and feel?

2. **Be Intelligent:** What does this experience suggest about what God is calling you to do? What does it say about those to whom you were ministering?

3. **Be Reasonable:** What past experiences led you to this ministry? How do these past experiences affect your current understanding? What other meanings are possible? Does the forgotten detail suggest a new insight about the meaning of your experience?

4. **Be Responsible:** Does this experience lead you to new ministries or to deepen your commitment to this ministry?

5. **Be in Love Transformed:** What do you need to make this change or deepen your commitment? Ask God for new possibilities or new opportunities to practice to fulfill your ministry.

Chapter Eight

Spirituality: Created for Prayer

CREATED TO BE IN RELATIONSHIP

At a traffic light I sensed to my left a driver looking my way. He buzzed his window down and leaned toward me. I looked toward him. "I feel like I should be asking you if you have any Grey Poupon," he said. I returned his smile, acknowledging his allusion to the 1985 TV commercial. He continued, "But I'm looking for Route 22."

Common ground was a whimsical commercial for mustard. How little It takes. Were it not for traffic and schedules, we might have entered into conversation, perhaps lunch. A relationship might have blossomed.

Some fifteen years ago, I arranged for the installation of a large movable satellite dish on the bell tower of the Cathedral Church of the Nativity in Bethlehem, Pennsylvania. The local daily took photos. The published photo was taken at an opportune moment. As the crane lifted the dish three-quarters of the way, the cross at the peak of the facade of the adjoining building was clearly visible through the dish.

A few years later, on my drive to work, at a point where I should have merged onto the thruway and made it to Diocesan House in time for Morning Prayer, I continued instead toward Dunkin' Donuts. I thought I needed coffee and a donut more than Morning Prayer. As I sat at the counter previewing my day, a car crashed through the plate glass wall. I spun on my stool and touched its hood. No one was hurt. Later, I found in my jacket pocket a handful of pebbles from the tempered glass.

I have framed those incidents into a prayerful practice on my drive to work. I pray first about connection and relationships. Then, mortality. Finally, as I begin to cross a bridge where traffic slows and the Cathedral Church comes into view, I look for the cross and the satellite dish.

That image in search of a theology of communication centers me. The cross of the one great Mediator, Jesus Christ, is a window into the heart of God. This God is far beyond my limited imagination. It's hard to believe in a God who loves us before we do anything, and who continues to love and reach out to us even after we do whatever we think puts us beyond God's graceful embrace.

My eyes and mind wander toward the satellite dish, barely visible, searching heaven and earth for many other media of God's self-disclosure. God is still speaking.

Where will God show up today? Is God counting on me to show up, to mediate God's love?

That spiritual exercise, crafted from a trinity of experiences, works for me.

Brother Martin Smith once said that some words we commonly use "cry out to be partnered with other words." One is incomplete without the other. Spirituality seems to me to cry out for at least three words: "relationship," "mission," and "transformation."

Our inner journey of spirituality focuses on relationship—with God, with our sisters and brothers, and with all of God's creation. It works itself out in what might be called our public journey of mission. Throughout, it yearns for transformation.

Crucial for Episcopal Christian spirituality is that we seek our personal fit among the classic practices and disciplines outlined in this chapter. Also crucial, lest we make the mistake of acting as though spirituality is a go-it-alone enterprise, is that we center our spirituality—our relationships, our mission, and our personal transformation—in our community celebration of Eucharist.

Limiting spirituality to pious practices or ethereal reflection gives spirituality a bad name and a not-so-spiritually positive outcome. It is normal for spirituality to simmer in mind and heart, prompted likely by personal experiences, but it must continually get down, waist deep, in history.

You may know the quip about how to make God laugh. Tell God your plans. There's another about how to bore God. Limit your spirituality to pious practices.

We are created to be in relationship. This mystery may be our best clue to reality. We need others: to be and to become.

That we are so created reaches deeply into the mystery we call Trinity, the name our Christian tradition has given to the shared, giving, loving life together of God whom we invoke as Father/Mother, Son, and Holy Spirit.

God's "is" — being-in-relationship, being-in-community — trickles down. Everything that rests not on relationship, even beliefs, rests on sand.   **—B.L.**

◆ ◆ ◆

A RELATIONSHIP WITH GOD

Bill describes how experiences of a single day have been transformed into a meaningful practice of prayer. Your life, too, calls you into prayer, a relationship with God. Our God loves us deeply and is constantly calling us closer. The Bible is filled with examples of God's lives being transformed into prayer. God asked Noah to build an ark. Abraham negotiated with God to save the city of Sodom. Hannah asked God for a son. Moses spoke with God many times — revealing his own weaknesses and telling God, "I can't do it." Jesus was always talking with God. In fact, we might say that Jesus lived a life of unceasing prayer.

What does it mean that Jesus lived a life of unceasing prayer? Well, Jesus spent time alone and in silence, an activity many of us easily identify as prayer. One example is when Jesus went up the mountains by himself after feeding the five thousand who had come to hear him preach (Matthew 14). But a life of unceasing prayer is more than getting away from it all now and then. It's acknowledging God's presence in all that we do. It is living a life of transformation in close relationship with God.

"Pray without ceasing," the apostle Paul urges us in 1 Thessalonians 5:17. Be attentive to the rhythm of your life. Is there a discernible pattern, or are your days chaotic? Try to understand how you might "pray without ceasing." Which of the practices that follow might best enable you to be in relationship with God throughout your day?

The Book of Common Prayer defines **prayer** this way: "Prayer is responding to God, by thought and deeds, with or without words." So our actions in the world, our ministry, are prayers. Since we explored ministry in the last chapter, we will explore other forms of prayer here.

In the introduction to this chapter Bill shares how a trinity of experiences was transformed into a daily prayer. What experiences of yours beg to be transformed into prayer?

Jesus spent most of his years of ministry among people, studying, fasting, celebrating, worshiping, and being in fellowship with others. These are all *spiritual disciplines* that support a life of unceasing prayer. **Spiritual disciplines** are intentional practices that keep us in dialogue with God. Spiritual disciplines reinforce a life of unceasing prayer — and are also the result of unceasing prayer.

A number of spiritual disciplines can bring you to a closer relationship with God. We are not meant to practice all the disciplines all the time. Some are appropriate for particular seasons of the year. Lent, for example, is a season of fasting, while Easter is a season of celebration. Be attentive to your experience. Not every discipline suits every person. It's like any other activity: you might love to hike in the mountains while your best friend might be happiest swimming in the ocean. Be intelligent: take a look at each of the spiritual practices that follow, and be reasonable: decide which ones might help you find a closer relationship with God.

CONVERSATIONS WITH GOD

When we talk with friends, we generally talk about the many different things happening in our lives. Sometimes we share a hurt or celebration. At other times we might say how much we appreciate their friendship or give them a compliment. If we have hurt a friend, we might ask for forgiveness to restore our friendship. Our conversations with God are just as real and just as diverse.

The principal kinds of prayer are adoration, confession, thanksgiving, intercession, and petition. A good way to remember them is the acronym ACTIP,[19] one letter for each of the five fingers on your hand. Prayers of **adoration** are words and actions that express our love for God and creation. An example is the Gloria during Eucharist when we sing or say "Glory to God in the highest." We ask for nothing; we just praise God's presence.

In a prayer of **confession** we admit that we have done something wrong, turn away from sin, and seek to restore our relationship with others through God. An example of a prayer of confession is the general confession during worship in which we say, "We have not loved you with our whole heart. . . . We are truly sorry and we humbly repent."

When we express our gratitude to God for all the blessings and mercies God gives us, we are offering a prayer of **thanksgiving**. Before the evening meal our family thanks God for food and drink and the day.

Intercessions are requests for God's blessings and healing grace for others. The Prayers of the People — when we pray for the church, our nation, the world, our community, people in trouble, and those who have died — are prayers of intercession.

Prayers of **petition** are requests for God's blessings and grace for ourselves. We might ask God for guidance in making a decision, protection from evil, or the healing of pain.

We can pray in other ways than words. Kneeling in confession or lifting up our hands in praise are prayers too. When you pray, you don't have to include a prayer of every type. Let your heart guide your prayer.

THE DAILY OFFICE

The **Daily Office** in the Book of Common Prayer provides a disciplined way of acknowledging God's presence in our lives through daily prayer and readings. (Morning Prayer begins on page 35 of the Book of Common Prayer.) With Morning Prayer we declare the day sacred and invite God to begin the day

19. Anne E. Kitch, *The Anglican Family Prayer Book* (Harrisburg, Pa.: Morehouse Publishing, 2004), 61.

The Monastic Horaria (Hours)

Matins and Lauds	daybreak
Prime, the first hour	6:00 a.m.
Terce, the third hour	9:00 a.m.
Sext, the sixth hour	noon
None, the ninth hour	3:00 p.m.
Vespers	sunset
Compline	bedtime

with us. In the morning hours of new light we look forward to the day, praising God, maker of heaven and earth. As the sun sets we turn to Evening Prayer to reflect on the day and thank God for providing a Savior, a light to enlighten the nations.

Setting aside time each day for prayer and study gives us the opportunity to invite God into our daily routine, to recognize that God is continually at work in our lives, and to respond to God's presence with praise and thanksgiving. The practice of setting aside time each day for study and prayer dates back to the times of the Jewish scriptures. The Hebrews said the *Shema,* a declaration of faith, two or three times a day. Psalm 119 says "Seven times a day I praise you." Jesus and the disciples prayed daily, and so did early Christian communities.

Early Christian communities continued the Jewish practice of marking their days with prayer. In the early centuries of the church, some Christians organized and lived in **monastic communities.** A monastic community is a group of Christians who live apart from society and dedicate themselves to simple lives of study, prayer, and service ordered by a rule. Early communities developed seven Daily Offices, or times of prayer, beginning with Lauds (morning prayer) upon waking and ending with Compline before going to sleep. See the box above for a list.

The Daily Offices in our prayer book are based on these monastic offices. Just as in the monastic offices, in both Evening and Morning Prayer are the psalms, scripture, and prayers. We call these elements the Invitatory and Psalter, the Lessons, and the Prayers. The **Invitatory** is a sentence and response that invites our hearts and minds to the purpose of the gathering. In Morning Prayer, for example, we say,

Officiant	Lord, open our lips.
People	And our mouth shall proclaim your praise.

And at Evening Prayer we begin with:

Officiant	O God, make speed to save us.
People	O Lord, make haste to help us.

Notice the difference in the tone between Morning and Evening Prayer. At day's break we begin with praise and thank God for the coming day. After the day has passed, we ask for God's forgiveness, knowing that we have fallen short of what God calls us to do. We ask for forgiveness even though God has already forgiven us before the day began.

In the morning the Invitatory and Psalter continue with an antiphon, the Venite or Jubilate, and a psalm. **Antiphons** are sentences, usually from the Bible, that we say before and after the psalm. The Venite (Psalm 95:1–7) and the Jubilate (Psalm 100) invite us to rejoice in the God of creation and praise God's goodness. In the evening we say the Phos Hilaron ("O Gracious Light"), which acknowledges the day has ended, but continues to be filled with the light that God brought into the world through Jesus Christ.

A psalm is known by its opening phrase in Latin. Psalm 121 is called *Levavi oculos* because its first phrase is "I lift up my eyes."

Both offices continue with a psalm followed by one or more lessons. You can find the cycle of appointed psalms and readings in the back pages of the Book of Common Prayer, beginning on page 934. If you follow the cycle of psalms and readings for the two-year cycle, you will have read a lot of the Bible. After the lessons we say a **canticle** (a "little song" based on scripture), and the Apostles' Creed. The traditional canticles for Evening Prayer are the Magnificat, the song of Mary in Luke's story of the birth of Jesus, and the Nunc Dimittis, the song of Simeon when he saw the Christ Child, also in Luke's Gospel. Both canticles acknowledge God's greatness and gift of salvation through Jesus Christ.

The final element of both offices are the prayers. These prayers have four parts: the Lord's Prayer, suffrages, collect, and intercessions and thanksgivings. With the prayers we give thanks and ask God to remember our needs as well as the needs of our community, both close by and around the world.

Both Evening and Morning Prayer have optional beginnings: an opening sentence of scripture, confession, and absolution. Evening Prayer can also begin with "The Service of Light," which focuses on the fading of the day and acknowledges that even the darkness is radiant in God's sight.

The Book of Common Prayer offers two additional daily prayers: Noonday Prayer, said at midday, and Compline, said just before turning into bed for the night. For those whose days do not have room for these liturgies, the prayer book provides briefer "Daily Devotions for Individuals and Families" (pages 136–40). Whether you pray the Daily Offices alone or in a group, when you pray, you pray with many other Christians around the world.

SILENCE AND LISTENING

Prayer is a conversation. It requires the presence of you and God. God is always with us, but we aren't always aware of it. Most of us aren't in tune with God's presence. We think prayer is telling God all about ourselves and often we allow little time for God to talk to us. Imagine the possibility that God is speaking to us, calling to us, asking us for something, or praising us. Conversations are, after all, two-way. By hogging the conversation, we hardly give God time to talk. The spiritual exercises below will help you listen to what God has to say and offer your own words now and then, too.

Centering Prayer (Listening beyond Words)

Have you ever been in love? At first, you want to be with the other person all the time. What you do doesn't seem to matter — talking or just sitting quietly together is enough. Just being in the presence of the other is fulfilling. That is how it is with God. But the difference is that God is with us *always,* even though we are not always aware of it. While the world might seem to be physically separate from God, just as the air we breathe is all around and inside us, but unseen, so is God. Feeling the presence of God, the one who loves you fully, is like taking a deep breath. God fills our entire being.

Like the spiritual life itself, prayer is initiated by God. No matter what we think about the origin of our prayers, they are all a response to the hidden workings of the spirit within. —Marjorie Thompson[20]

Centering prayer is a prayer of quieting and stillness that lets you know the presence of God in your innermost parts. It is a prayer without words and a journey to the center of your being.

20. Marjorie Thompson, *Soul Feast* (Louisville: Westminster John Knox Press, 2005), 3.

Centering Prayer: The Practice

First, find a quiet and comfortable place to sit. Choose a sacred word that gives God permission to be present and act within you. Common sacred words are "God," "Jesus," "Amma," or "Father." Choose a word that reflects the love of God, but one that brings forth the fewest images — either positive or negative. The idea is to empty yourself of thought. The word itself is not important. It's just a word that says you're ready for God.

Close your eyes and introduce the sacred word gently. As thoughts, feelings, or images surface, gently acknowledge them and let them go. An image that may be helpful is a stream. As you see thoughts of the day approach, don't be alarmed. Gently let them continue down the stream. Centering prayer is not a prayer of words, but a silent prayer to God to whom "all hearts are open, all desires known, and from [whom] no secrets are hid" (Book of Common Prayer, page 355). God knows our needs and answers our prayers before they are even asked.

Your body may twitch or itch during centering prayer. This is your body's way of working through its stress. If this distracts you, repeat your sacred word gently. You don't have to say the word constantly. When you notice that your mind is wandering or thoughts are getting in the way, reintroduce the word. As you continue, you will find a peacefulness within yourself. Rest in that peace. Don't worry if thoughts interrupt that peace. If they do, gently say your sacred word and let the thought go by.

Centering prayer has its beginnings with the Desert Fathers and Mothers — Christians who lived in the deserts of Egypt during the fourth and fifth centuries and followed a life of solitude and self-discipline. This form of prayer was the primary way of prayer for monks for centuries, and more people have become interested in it today, thanks to the writings of modern-day Trappist monk Thomas Keating.

The practice is simple. If you've ever entered a church and sat down quietly to prepare for a service, you've begun the practice of centering prayer. Its simple form, however, hides how difficult it can be in practice — and its rich rewards.

A good image of how centering prayer works is to imagine that you are stepping into a holy circle. The circle is separated from the busyness of the day, and at the center is God. You journey in a continually inward spiral away from your thoughts and the noise of the day toward the center of yourself — and God. Keep this image of the circle in mind as you try centering prayer.

Practicing contemplative prayer for ten minutes a day is a good beginning. To mark your time, choose quiet music to begin playing on your mp3 or CD player after ten minutes. Or set a timer to ring gently after ten minutes. If you have a computer, you can use the meditation at *www.contemplativeprayer.net* to set your time. When your time of stillness is over, come out of the stillness by reciting the Lord's Prayer.

The fruit of centering prayer is knowing that God deeply yearns for you, God's beloved. Centering prayer is not meditation in a void. It is creating empty spaces deep within to allow the Holy Spirit to grow inside. You will be amazed: knowing God's love and deep presence will help you to see God in all of creation and to respond to God's creation with loving actions.

Mantras

Inviting God to be with you is the beginning of any prayer. Some people find saying **mantras** — sacred words or phrases said repeatedly for a period of time — helps quiet their body and mind and invites God to be with them.

An example of a simple mantra is "Come, Holy Spirit, Come." This simple mantra names the presence of the divine and invites God to be with you. Another mantra is the **Jesus Prayer**: Lord, Jesus Christ, son of God, have mercy on me, a sinner.

breathe in saying	Lord, Jesus Christ,
breathe out saying	son of God,
breathe in saying	have mercy on me,
breathe out saying	a sinner

A final example is the **Trisagion**, a Latin word that means "thrice holy": Holy God, Holy and Mighty, Holy Immortal One, Have mercy on me.

breathe in saying	Holy God
breathe out saying	Holy and Mighty
breathe in saying	Holy Immortal One
breathe out saying	Have mercy on me

Mantras: The Practice

Find a quiet place to sit and get comfortable. Be sure to remain sitting up and attentive. You want to be relaxed so that you are aware, but not so relaxed that you fall asleep. Take a deep breath in and say, "Come, Holy Spirit." Say it aloud. Breathe out saying "Come."

> *breathe in saying*   "Come, Holy Spirit"
> *breathe out saying*   "Come "

Repeat this cycle of breathing in and out with the words "Come, Holy Spirit, Come" for five minutes. At the end of your prayer, stay in the silence for a few minutes and notice where your heart leads you. At the end of your prayer, thank God for your time together. "Come, Holy Spirit" is one mantra. The text offers two other examples.

The Jesus Prayer and the Trisagion, like the words "Come, Holy Spirit, Come," invite God and Jesus Christ to be present in our hearts. Repeating the words of invitation begins to empty your heart and mind, providing room for the Holy Spirit to grow.

The result of this prayer is intimacy with God, a closeness that reveals that God provides every need. For some the gift is knowing that we are loved, for others a protection from evil, and still others a depth of love that gives us permission to offer our sins and be forgiven. Each of us has a unique and important relationship with God that deepens with prayer.

If it's difficult to remain physically still for longer than five minutes, that's okay. We are, after all, physical beings. If you quickly become restless you might find it helpful to use Anglican prayer beads along with a mantra.

Anglican Prayer Beads

Anglican prayer beads — sometimes called the rosary — are a set of thirty-three beads joined together in a circular pattern. You hold them in your hands and say sacred words as you travel with your fingers around the string of beads. Because it adds a physical element to prayer, the rosary engages our mind, spirit, and body. Fingering successive beads creates a focus for sometimes fidgety hands and links that focus to the words of our lips. In addition, the structure of the rosary and repetitive action of the beads creates a rhythm for prayer that stills our hearts.

The Origin of Beads. Beads were first used for prayer in the second century B.C.E. by followers of the Hindu faith as a way of counting prayers. The practice spread to Buddhism, Islam, and finally to Christianity. In the mid-sixteenth century Pope Pius V decreed that St. Dominic, founder of the Dominican Order, invented the rosary and the classic form for the Roman Catholic rosary. Leaders of the Protestant Reformation discouraged people from using rosaries for devotions, and today rosaries are most commonly associated with the Roman Catholic Church. The pattern we know as Anglican prayer beads developed in the 1980s. It has a cross, an invitatory bead, and twenty-eight beads divided into four weeks by four cruciform beads.

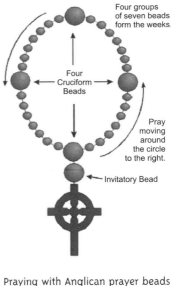

Four groups of seven beads form the weeks.

Four Cruciform Beads

Pray moving around the circle to the right.

Invitatory Bead

Praying with Anglican prayer beads is a way to include your body in prayer.

The modern word "bead" comes from the old English word *bede,* meaning prayer. A bedesman was someone whose duty it was to pray for others.

The Symbolism of Anglican Prayer Beads. The structure of Anglican prayer beads is richly symbolic, connecting our prayer with time and space. Each of four groups of seven beads is called a *week.* The number seven reminds us of the seven days of our week, the seven days of creation, and the seven sacraments. In Jewish and Christian traditions, the number seven represents perfection and completion. The weeks are divided by four larger beads called *cruciform beads.* The four cruciform beads form the points of a cross, reminding us that by Jesus' death and resurrection we are freed from the power of sin and reconciled to God. Dividing the beads into groups of four also reminds us of the four seasons of the year and the four directions on a compass. The circular pattern symbolizes a journey and reminds us that the cycles of life — joy, sorrow, birth, and death — often repeat themselves.

In Anglican prayer beads earthly and divine symbols are intertwined, reminding us that our souls and bodies are intimately connected: our faith involves our bodies too. God came to earth as a human being to be among us. Jesus suffered on the cross and rose from the dead. We live our faith as the body of Christ in the world — a physical world with days, seasons, and geography — all made sacred by God.

Prayer beads are meant to help you pray. At first, remembering the words might be difficult and the beads might be confusing. Relax. Start with simple prayers — perhaps only two: one for the weeks and one for all other beads. With practice you will become more comfortable. Trust your intuition; other prayer practices might better help create the space where you and God can meet.

Anglican Prayer Beads: The Practice

We often use prayer beads along with words. Before you begin, choose four simple prayers. Two of the prayers are said as you enter the circle — one for the cross and another for the invitatory, or first, bead. A simple prayer for the cross is, "In the Name of God the Father, Son, and Holy Spirit, Amen." You might try using the Trisagion for the invitatory bead and the cruciform beads and the Jesus Prayer for the weeks.

As you enter the circle, move to the right saying the Jesus Prayer for each of the seven beads, followed by the Trisagion for the cruciform bead, and returning to the Jesus Prayer. Going around the entire rosary three times before ending with the invitatory and cross represents the Trinity of the Father, Son, and Holy Spirit. By the end of three rounds, you will have said one hundred prayers. More than that, you will find your heart to be still and your mind to be at rest. Before completing your time of prayer, spend some time in silence and thank God for being with you.

Lectio Divina

As Christians we believe that the Bible is the revealed word of God. God inspired human authors who wrote the texts through which God speaks. So a natural place to listen to God's voice is the Bible. People read the Bible in many ways — for its literary value, for instruction, for inspiration. The first two kinds of reading use the human intellect and invite us to study the history, translation, and setting of the Bible stories. The third way requires

---

Lectio Divina: **The Practice**

Lectio divina has four steps: reading, meditating, praying, and contemplating. To begin, find a place where you can listen quietly and select a brief passage from the Bible. Quiet your body and your mind with slow breathing. Perhaps say a mantra. (See page 133.)

Read. Read the passage slowly, savoring each word and allowing the words to sink deeply into your inner self. Ask yourself, "What word or phrase is speaking to me right now?" This question helps you to hear God's still small voice speaking to you softly, gently, and in love.

Meditate. Take that word and recite it over and over again. This step is meditation. Open your heart to that word. It is a gift from God. Let your thoughts and imagination play with the word. What images does the word suggest? What thoughts or desires surface within you? By meditating on the word God has given you, you can find the word to be part of you.

Pray. Now let the word touch you deeply. Pray with the word. What feelings and emotions does this word bring to mind? Hold these feelings gently, without judgment, and repeat the word. Hold yourself up to God for God's healing grace and guidance.

Contemplate. Finally, rest in God's love. Accept God's loving embrace. Enjoy God's presence and thank God for the gift you have received. This final step is called contemplation.

us to listen with our hearts to what the word of God is saying to each of us personally at that particular moment.

One way of this deep listening to scripture is *lectio divina* (Latin for divine reading). Specifically, **lectio divina** is a four-step process of prayerfully reading the word of God. See the box on the previous page for the steps. St. Benedict, a Christian monk who lived in the fifth century C.E. and who believed reading and study are a central part of a sacred life, encouraged a widespread practice of *lectio divina*.

Lectio divina is not meant to replace the study of scripture. Studying scripture with commentaries helps us to understand the communities and times when the stories and poetry in the Bible were written. It helps us interpret the Bible with the insights of scholars.

The process of *lectio divina* can also be used with poems, pictures, objects from nature, or life events. God speaks to us today through the created world as well as through the Bible. Follow the four steps for *lectio divina*, but instead of focusing on a word, focus on the subject you have chosen. Doing this will help you begin to see all of God's creation as sacred.

Praying through Icons

Some people like to use visual images when they pray, and icons are great images to pray with. **Icons** are visual images that point beyond themselves.

Rublev's fourteenth-century Russian icon of the Trinity invites the viewer into a relationship.

They can be powerful instruments that instruct us, changing our behavior and attitude. The Nike logo with its message "just do it" is just one of the many icons in our culture. It tells people to get moving and do something. The image of George Washington printed on a dollar bill is another American icon. That icon tells us that this little green piece of paper is valuable. We can give it to a clerk at a store, and the clerk will give us the product we've chosen. The power of an icon comes from what they represent or point to. George Washington's image on the dollar represents trust — trust that this piece of paper can be exchanged for something real. Icons are everywhere. The images on your computer screen are also icons. "Clicking" on these icons launches powerful programs that perform many functions. Holy icons are similar. They point beyond themselves to the Holy and lead us into the powerful presence of God. Traditional icons are beautiful paintings of Jesus, Mary, the mother of Jesus, and the saints — holy men and women who have gone before us. These icons are "written" by artists in prayer. Find an icon. Notice that it has an inner light that invites you to gaze at it patiently and prayerfully. Icons also have movement — a movement from the viewer inward to the people in the icon, inviting you into a relationship with God.

Icons don't have to be painted. Nature is filled with icons that point to God our Creator: a dandelion, a blade of grass, a bird's nest. Although all of them serve a purpose in nature, they are also beautiful images pointing to their Creator. Taking the time to read these icons can show us the beauty of creation. Consider the hexagonal honeycomb. The fact that it both incubates bees and stores food with mathematical beauty reveals an immensely complex and creative Creator.

> The heavens are telling the glory of God.... There is no speech, nor are there words, their voice is not heard; yet their voice goes out through all the earth, and their words to the end of the world.
>
> (Psalm 19:1, 3–4)

How can you pray through an icon? First select an icon — either by going to where it is (in nature) or by bringing it to a sacred place indoors. Focus your gaze on the icon. Begin by quieting your body, mind, and spirit. Ask God to be present and focus on the beauty and inner life of the icon. What is the icon saying about itself? What is it saying about God? What feeling does the icon evoke in you? Focus on and rest with this feeling. Respond to God as you are moved — with adoration, confession, thanksgiving, intercession, or praise. End with a familiar prayer such as the Lord's Prayer.

PRAYING WITH YOUR BODY

So far, we've talked about prayer without words, with words, and with images. In each of these practices — except with Anglican prayer beads — our bodies have not been active participants. We are physical beings and God loves all of who we are, so our worship and prayer practices reflect that fact. During our worship, for example, we kneel or stand for prayer. Many people make the sign of the cross and bow as the cross is processed by.

 Our bodies hold memories. Kneel or take your common position of prayer. Does this change how you feel or what you are thinking?

These motions hold **ritual memory** — the remembering of actions that deepen our experiences as they are repeated. An example of ritual memory is kneeling in prayer. Try it. Because we have done it so often our act of kneeling places our minds and bodies in the context of prayer. When we kneel our bodies remember other times we have knelt — the emotions, smells, sights, and sounds that surrounded us while kneeling. Ritual memory is powerful. So be mindful of our bodies and prayer. The following practices engage other parts of our bodies in prayer.

Mandalas

Creating visual images while we invite God to be present can be a powerful way to pray. Being creative with our hands focuses our minds and hearts and allows us to explore our innermost selves. Many people reveal themselves best by doodling, drawing, painting, or coloring.

This mandala is from an Egyptian liturgical fan used to keep insects away from the bread and wine.

One visual method of prayer is to draw a **mandala,** a circular pattern of lines and colors. You can find mandalas throughout nature. The cell with its nucleus, the nautilus, the earth seen from space, and the pattern of our spiraling galaxy, even the atom, are all mandalas. The stained-glass rose windows in many churches and the labyrinth are also mandalas. Because a circle has no beginning or end, mandalas represent the wholeness of creation at the cosmic and micro levels. The circle creates a safe place within which we can reconcile our feelings and thoughts with God.

Mandalas have a long history. Buddhist monks in ancient Tibet began the practice of creating mandalas by making beautiful and intricate circular patterns with sand. The word "mandala" comes from the Sanskrit word that means circle.

Mandalas: The Practice

To begin, draw a large circle with a compass on a large blank sheet of paper. Actively invite God to the circle and to your prayer. Let your thoughts and emotions suggest a color and pattern and begin to draw. Let your imagination go with pencils, paints, crayons, magic markers, and other drawing tools. Draw what comes to mind—there is no "right" or "wrong" mandala. Each mandala is unique. Empty yourself into the circle, offering your worries, thoughts, hopes, and desires to God.

Twelfth-century German mystic Hildegard von Bingen, known for her visions and musical and artistic abilities, created many mandalas.

Drawing a mandala is a way of paying attention to your inner self. When you have finished your mandala, look at it as a whole to see what themes emerge. Where is God in the pattern? After a period of reflection, give thanks to God for drawing you closer.

Journaling

Journaling is a discipline of putting our thoughts on paper as a way of reflection, self-examination, and prayer. Journals can free your inner voice to speak with raw honesty. Journaling can help you make sense of where your life is headed, work out complicated thoughts and feelings, and understand what God is calling you to do. Journals are meant to free the soul. They can be filled with words, drawings, and doodles. Pour your stories and feelings out. They often reflect our innermost hopes, fears, anger, and love.

> Every person has an inner voice. Journaling can often help us hear it more clearly.

As with any kind of prayer, journaling is personal. You can journal in spiral-bound notebooks, on the computer, or in a scrapbook. Begin by inviting God to your journaling. Be attentive to your experiences. Be honest, even if it is painful or you think that God doesn't want to hear it. Without honesty you cannot truly face yourself or God. Writing will help you find your own voice. Seeing your thoughts on paper helps to recognize your own authority. Try it.

Written words have a permanence not matched by spoken words and remain for you to read and reread. You might notice that when you return to past entries your thoughts are different than you remember or have changed. Reading past thoughts will help you identify those changes in your life. If you cannot find words to write, try journaling with images. Perhaps journaling with mandalas will help you hear your inner voice.

God speaks to us through our lives. Ask yourself where God is in your journal. What is God saying to you? Journaling can bring our lives together and remember its parts so that we can see its wholeness with common themes, questions, and directions. Journaling can help you be aware of God's transforming work in your life. As you close your journal, offer what you have written to God.

Walking a Labyrinth

A **labyrinth** is a sacred pattern in the shape of a circle with one path that winds to the center and back out again. With its circular shape of a mandala, the labyrinth reflects the unity and wholeness of creation and our lives.

A particularly famous labyrinth is the eleven-circuit labyrinth on the floor of the Chartres Cathedral in France. This labyrinth was built in the twelfth century for Christian pilgrimages. The Crusades had made pilgrimages to Jerusalem, Rome, and Santiago dangerous, and the church designated seven cathedrals in France, including Chartres, as alternate pilgrimage destinations. After arriving, pilgrims would walk the labyrinth before receiving the Eucharist.

The labyrinth is a mandala that you walk to pray.

Lauren Artress, a priest at Grace Cathedral in San Francisco, led the installation of the eleven-circuit labyrinth at Grace Cathedral and in the 1990s founded the modern labyrinth movement. Today, you can find labyrinths in nearly every major American city. Small finger labyrinths are available for people who are unable to walk, do not live near a floor labyrinth, or just like having a labyrinth at hand. You can also find labyrinths on the Internet.

Just like any journey, walking a labyrinth can be transformational. Once you enter the labyrinth, you begin a journey that takes you to the center and out again. You can focus on taking the next step on the path with God, without worrying about the destination. Unlike a maze, which is designed to make us lost or confused, a labyrinth has no wrong turns and no dead ends. Because you don't have to use your brain to walk the labyrinth successfully, you can free your heart to listen to God. People who have walked labyrinths often say they find that God has given them an answer to an important question while they were on their labyrinth journey.

A labyrinth is a metaphor for life with a loving God who does not deceive or lead us astray. Walking the labyrinth is a journey with a God who calls us to a journey of wholeness.

Just like our real life, the journey on the labyrinth includes relationship with others. If you walk the labyrinth with a group, you will pass others along the way or brush the shoulders of people walking along other circuits. Sometimes you will be walking toward someone and other times away from someone. Everyone will be on the same path.

Fasting

Fasting is actively choosing not to do something for a short period of time so that we can draw our attention toward God. Often, fasting is associated with abstaining from food. For centuries the physical discipline of abstaining from food has been recognized as a way of developing self-control and of emptying oneself. At the time of Jesus, Jews fasted regularly. In the Gospel according to Matthew, Jesus fasted for forty days before beginning his ministry, and from historic writings we know that early Christians recognized Wednesdays and Fridays as fast days. Today, Lent — the forty days leading up to Easter — is a common time for Christians to practice the discipline of fasting.

By fasting we give up our physical attachment to material things and, just as in centering prayer, allow space for the Holy Spirit to enter us. It is not meant to be a time of deprivation nor is it meant to cause bodily harm. By removing food from our day, fasts can free us to center on God. By abstaining from food we allow our spiritual needs to take priority.

God is always trying to give good things to us, but our hands are too full to receive them. — St. Augustine

---

If you choose to fast from food, begin with a twenty-four-hour fast starting with lunch. With a normal fast, you abstain from food but continue to drink liquids such as water and juice. Begin by praying to God about when would be a good day to fast. Two fast days of the church are Ash Wednesday and Good Friday. Select a day you will not be particularly physically active.

Having the support of your family or community is especially helpful in a fast. Begin the day by eating breakfast. Skip snacking, lunch, and dinner. Remember, it is important to continue drinking liquids. Go about your day in inward prayer, thanking God for the tasks before you. When you find yourself reaching for the door of the refrigerator, remember your fast and God. The following morning, break your fast with a small meal and with thanksgiving.

Abstaining from food is not the only way to fast. If you want to fast, you might try fasting from television or the computer. Just remember, the intention of the fast is to take the time and energy previously dedicated to that activity and give it to prayer.

CELEBRATION

Birthdays are often cause for great celebration: a special meal of favorite foods, a cake, and gifts. Celebration, or feasting, is a way we mark life events. Celebration is also a spiritual discipline and part of a life of prayer.

The forty days of Lent, in which many practice fasting, is followed by a longer fifty days of Easter, a time of great celebration. After Jesus fasted for forty days, angels ministered to him. Celebration is a fundamental spiritual discipline. Does this surprise you? It shouldn't.

The very word "gospel" means good news. In the Gospel according to John, the first sign Jesus performed of the coming of the kingdom of God was turning water into wine at the wedding of Cana. Jesus uses the image of a banquet to describe God's kingdom. And in the face of his coming death, Jesus celebrates Passover, the liberation of the Jews from the Egyptians, with his closest friends. That death has been conquered and God's reign is near is cause for celebration!

The Eucharist that we celebrate every Sunday, in fact, is a celebration and *the* central act of the church. What marks celebration as a spiritual and prayerful act is that it is an intentional act of praise and thanksgiving that reflects our joy in God. We acknowledge that God is with us and mark the day with special foods and close friends.

Lesser Feasts and Fasts, a book that lists the church calendar with feast days that commemorate events of the life of Jesus as well as the lives of men and women who have dedicated their lives to active witness of God, gives us many opportunities for celebrating. This book includes collects, psalms, and lessons that you can read as part of a celebration at home. You might incorporate prayers and readings to the celebrations of God's abundance in *your* life.

RULE OF LIFE

Leading a spiritual life means developing an *ongoing* relationship with God. This chapter offers a number of spiritual disciplines to help you develop that relationship. But which ones will be good for *you?* How will they fit in with all the other things you have to do? Leading a spiritual life doesn't mean kneeling or drawing mandalas all day in prayer. We need to live balanced lives, with God at the center.

Maintaining a balance or even knowing what balance should look like isn't easy. Demands by others and by our egos get in the way. A helpful way to find and maintain balance is to develop a rule of life. A **rule of life** is a set of guidelines for living that helps us keep our lives in balance with God as its center.

Monastic communities live today — as they have for centuries — by rules of life. The best-known rule of life is the Rule of St. Benedict, written by Benedict of Nursia in the sixth century. The Rule of St. Benedict balances work and prayer and is guided by three overarching vows: stability, obedience, and conversion. The rule is a guide for monks on how to live in community. The box on the following page provides steps for developing your rule.

When a person joins a monastic community he or she vows to follow a rule of life that is different from other rules of life. For one, not everybody is called to a life of poverty or chastity, both common vows in monastic communities. Each of us is called by God to live a particular rule.

SPIRITUAL DIRECTION

Some people find spiritual direction helpful in developing an awareness of God in their lives. **Spiritual direction** is the art of helping others explore a deeper relationship with God. Spiritual directors are trained to listen deeply to others and to help listen to God and learn where God is leading them. They can help you develop an awareness of God working in your life and help you discern what spiritual disciplines will bring you closer to God. They are not therapists or problem solvers. They are holy listeners and wise people who can, with God, help guide you in creating a life of spiritual discipline that brings you closer to God.

DEVELOPING YOUR SPIRITUALITY

There are many more spiritual practices we didn't explore — retreats, simplicity, study, and service are just a few. With all of the possibilities of spiritual

Rule of Life: The Practice

Debra Farrington suggests making a list of activities that bring you joy as a way to begin to develop your rule of life. You may enjoy running, writing, drawing, reading, or spending time alone. This list is the beginning of your rule of life. Put your activities into five categories: work, study, prayer, play, and service to others. Study might be reading the Bible or books about the Christian tradition.

Bring this list to God and pray for guidance. You may begin to recognize for the first time that some activities are spiritual. Running, for example, takes care of your body and therefore is a way of returning the blessing of health to God. Time with friends and family creates a community of love and support. You may want to rebalance some parts of your life. If so, take on a discipline that is reasonable. A rule of life is a realistic set of guidelines.

Keep your rule of life handy. It will help you remain accountable and help you see when the rule needs to be modified. A rule of life is a living structure and will change. Most of all, a rule of life that makes God the center of your life is a blessing that can bring you into closer relationship to God.[21]

practices, you might wonder, "Where do I begin?" Begin with a prayer of petition from Psalm 19:14:

> Let the words of my mouth and the meditation of my heart
> be acceptable in your sight,
> O LORD, my rock and my redeemer.

Remember the parable of the sower in Matthew 13 and Mark 4? A sower sowed seeds. Some fell on a path, and the birds ate them up. Some fell on rocky ground. They sprang up, but the soil was too shallow and the plants

---

21. The categories of a rule of life and steps for creating rules is loosely based on "Balancing Life by the Rule," by Debra Farrington in *Spirituality and Health* (Winter 2001).

withered. Other seeds fell among thorns, and the thorns choked the plants. Some seeds fell on good soil and grew into an abundant harvest. If we till our lives and cultivate the spirit, God's love and blessings will grow abundantly. The fruits of the Spirit — love, joy, peace, patience, kindness, goodness, and faith — will be plentiful.

✠ TRANSFORMING QUESTIONS

1. **Be Attentive:** Describe a recent time when you prayed. (Remember, there are many ways to pray.) What was your prayer? What did you say or do? What did you hear and see?

2. **Be Intelligent:** What was the purpose of your prayer? Might there be other purposes? Let these other possibilities come to you without judgment.

3. **Be Reasonable:** Which purpose rings most true? What new insight does this bring to your understanding of prayer in general?

4. **Be Responsible:** In light of this experience, how might you change your practice of prayer?

5. **Be in Love Transformed:** What new ways of praying might you consider?

Chapter Nine

Worship:
Responding to God's Blessings

A THIN PLACE ON SUNDAY MORNING

"Thin places," in Celtic spirituality, are where ordinary reality and God's holiness meet, where we move easily between both realities, where the veil between heaven and earth seems transparent.

A thin place is anywhere our hearts are opened, according to theologian Marcus Borg. The Celts perceived the entire world as saturated with the glory of God. Though every place is potentially a thin place, we have to stop, look, and listen. We can, of course, be thick even about thin places—and not get it.

You may have experienced "thin places." Perhaps at Sunday worship: "Holy, holy, holy Lord...heaven and earth are full your glory....Blessed is he who comes in the name of the Lord." We gather for Eucharist that we might remember—tomorrow. That we might be sent. Worship is a "thin place."

"To fish," Robert Hughes writes in *A Jerk on One End: Reflections of a Mediocre Fisherman,* "you must notice things: the movement of the water and its patterns, the rocks, the seaweed...for fishing is intensely visual, even—perhaps especially—when nothing is happening. It is easy to look, but learning to see is a more gradual business, and it sneaks up on you unconsciously, by stealth. The sign that it is happening is the fact that you are not bored by the absence of the spectacular."

Might the absence of the spectacular help us discover our celebration of Eucharist as a "thin place"? It is a gradual experience—Sunday after Sunday—during which we are drawn from being attentive to learning how to see the spectacular in its apparent absence to deciding to "love one another as I have loved you," to serving the least of these, to being in Love transformed.

When you go to church on Sunday morning, do you expect to leave the same as you came? Do you expect that something will happen? Do you think your life may be transformed?

If we really understood the power we routinely invoke during Sunday worship, Annie Dillard suggests, we'd wear crash helmets in church.

If you have never experienced Sunday worship as a "thin place," you may be too pre-occupied. What is meant to occupy your attention in a "thin place" cannot, because your filled-up life crowds God out. There's no good reason that worship—when we gather the folks, break the bread, and share the stories—cannot be a "thin place."

Many voices vie for our attention, compete for our allegiance. Only one can lead us in the way of the really real. It is heard in thin times and places: "This is my Son. Listen to him."

Expect to hear God's voice. Expect that God will touch you. It happens. Be attentive. Somehow, somewhere, during your Sunday morning worship experience, expect God.

Getting tangled up with God will have implications you've not yet considered. Not simply an adjustment here, an adjustment there. Changes in the way you see and think and judge and do. Transformation. You will notice yourself living differently.

Bethlehem bishop Paul Marshall wrote of the premiere, at the Metropolitan Opera, of the new production of Puccini's *Turandot*. "What's interesting about the opera is another premiere. Puccini never finished *Turandot*. When he died in 1924, the opera was reverently finished by friends...from his notes."

At that premiere at La Scala in 1926, *Turandot* was conducted by Arturo Toscanini. When he came to the last passage Puccini had written, he put his baton down, and turned to the audience: "This is where the master ends," he announced. He then raised the baton and said, "This is where the friends continue."

In the movie *Chocolat,* a young priest preached at Easter: "We must measure our goodness, not by what we don't do, what we deny ourselves, what we resist, or whom we exclude. Instead, we should measure ourselves by what we embrace, what we create, and whom we include." After the Easter celebration and the chocolate festival in the town square, the town's control freak was "strangely released."

May we be released, transformed, through the death and resurrection of Jesus and through personal encounters with the risen Lord in all of our "thin places." May we be strangely released to do the master's work.   *—B.L.*

◆ ◆ ◆

Then God said, "Let us make humankind in our image, according to our likeness. (Genesis 1:26a)

God called order out of chaos by separating the heavens from the earth, the dry land from the sea, and distinguishing between the light of day and the light of night. God filled the earth with birds that fly, things that creep, monsters of the sea, plants yielding seed and trees bearing fruit. God said it was good. On the sixth day, God made humankind. And it was *very* good. We respond to the blessing of creation and God's continual blessings through history and our lives by worshiping God. **Worship** is a response of praise and thanksgiving to the God who created us, a God who knows us, blesses us each day, and wants to fulfill our heart's desires. We respond by giving our love and offering thanks. As created beings, it is our nature, as Bill says in the introduction, to enter the thin places where ordinary reality and God's holiness meet.

Worshiping God can be as simple as lighting a candle at home, saying a few words that tell God of our love, and giving thanks. Corporate worship gathers God's people who are scattered throughout the week to worship together. The Book of Common Prayer offers a number of ways to worship.

Be attentive as you worship with your faith community. Try to understand how worship and gospel imperatives are in dynamic relationship. If this seems not to be so in your life, why not? What might you do about that?

THE BOOK OF COMMON PRAYER

The Book of Common Prayer is the manual for community and personal worship in the Episcopal Church. It contains the words and actions, called

The Book of Common Prayer was first published in 1559.
This title page is from the 1662 Book of Common Prayer.

liturgies, that define our common worship as a community. The word "liturgy" comes from the Greek word *liturgeia*, which means "public work." In church life everyone contributes his or her part to the community's ministry. Liturgy is something people do, not something people watch. In the Episcopal Church, the liturgy is truly the work and words of the people. The words of the Sunday liturgy are shared by all Episcopalians and reflect the theology of our community. Every Sunday, Anglican churches throughout the world follow similar forms of worship.

Liturgy is powerful. It expresses our beliefs, as well as shapes them. Consider Eucharist. When the priest gives us the communion bread saying, "The body of Christ, the bread of heaven," and we respond with "Amen," we receive Christ as spiritual food for our lives today. By eating the bread of heaven we partake in God's promised kingdom, and we leave the table transformed and strengthened to be the body of Christ in the world. Although we may repeat the same beautiful words and actions of the liturgy week after week, no liturgy is the same. When we return to the communion table we bring with us the experience of having lived as the body of Christ during the week. We are different people; we are fed again, and our belief in Christ's work in the world through us deepens. Liturgy transforms us.

Liturgy transforms us. How might you approach Sunday worship expecting a transformation so dramatic that you would be wise to wear a crash helmet?

Knowing when to use various liturgies and what to do within them can be complicated. The Book of Common Prayer includes rules and directions for the variety of services. "Concerning the Service of the Church" (13) describes the regular services appointed for public worship and who participates in those services. A similar page precedes most services. "The Calendar of the Church Year" (15–33) lists principal feasts, lesser feasts, and holy days, as well as the liturgical seasons. Moreover, each service provides directions for the ceremony in italics called **rubrics**.

The Book of Common Prayer also has the complete 150 psalms from the Hebrew scriptures (which we call the Old Testament), prayers and thanksgivings for a variety of occasions, an outline of the faith, historical documents of the church, tables to find the date of Easter and other holy days, and the lectionary.

HOLY EUCHARIST

So those who welcomed his message were baptized, and that day about three thousand persons were added. They devoted themselves to the apostles' teaching and fellowship, to the breaking of the bread and the prayers.

(Acts 2:41–42)

Our principal act of Christian worship, **Holy Eucharist**, follows the model of the early church — teaching and fellowship, breaking of the bread, and prayers. We celebrate Eucharist on Sundays and other major feast days such as Ash Wednesday. Many Christians celebrate Eucharist every day. The word "Eucharist" comes from the Greek word *eucharistia*, meaning "the giving of thanks." In the Eucharist we remember the life, death, and resurrection of Jesus Christ and proclaim that we await his coming again in glory. Through the Eucharist we are strengthened and nourished for our lives today and are given a foretaste of God's heavenly banquet. The Eucharist is a celebration by God's family of God's love for us.

The first Christians were Jews and God-fearing gentiles who worshiped in synagogues. So it should be no surprise that the framework of our service is based on synagogue services. Nehemiah 8 describes a service with readings from the Law of Moses and an exposition of the reading by the priest followed by a meal. Our service has similar parts: the Liturgy of the Word, during which we hear the word of God read and proclaimed, and the Liturgy of the Table, during which we take, bless, break, and give the bread and wine of communion.

LITURGY OF THE WORD

We are a people scattered throughout the world into different activities and locations, but we gather as one to worship. So it shouldn't be surprising that the Liturgy of the Word begins with a brief entrance rite that focuses our minds and hearts toward God and one another as a community of faith. During the opening hymn the acolytes, choir, deacons, priests, and bishop process through the people to their places to lead worship. It is important to note that the procession is through the people because worshiping God is the work of the people. All are members of Christ, equal but with different gifts.

Once everyone is in place, the celebrant continues with the **opening acclamation**, a greeting to God's family; we then sing the **Gloria**, a song of praise to God. The entrance rite ends with a **collect**, a short prayer that "collects" the themes of the day.

The order of the opening procession is a matter of tradition. The cross or Gospel Book often leads the procession, followed by the choir, and ending with the priest and, if present, the bishop. The procession reminds us that Christian life is a pilgrimage.

Try writing a collect for grace one evening at supper. Use what happened to you that day to respond to these prompts: "God who..." "I ask for..." "So that..."

We believe that God is present in both word and sacrament. Both nourish our lives as a people of God. We are fed in the Liturgy of the Word nourished by hearing stories from the Bible about God's redeeming acts throughout history. This portion of the liturgy generally includes four readings, although rubrics allow for three: a Jewish scripture reading, a recitation from the Psalms, a reading from the Epistles, and a reading from the Gospels. The readings are prescribed by a three-year cycle called the **lectionary**. In year A we read from the Gospel according to Matthew, in year B from Mark, and in year C from Luke. Readings from the Gospel according to John are interspersed throughout each of the three years, especially during the year that the Gospel according to Mark is read. The Epistles are read in sequence and the Jewish scripture readings are chosen to complement either the Gospel or Epistle readings. During Easter the Acts of the Apostles may be read in place of the Jewish scriptures. Having a lectionary means that every Episcopal church can read the same scriptures on any given Sunday.

By following a lectionary, we are challenged to understand sometimes contradictory writings and events. We cannot just keep to our favorite verses. We must grapple with the difficulty of interpretation and application of a wide variety of beliefs about God. By including the Jewish scriptures we are reminded that the roots of Christianity are in Judaism and that the God of the Jewish scriptures is the same God as in the Christian scriptures. Without the Jewish scripture we would not have a complete understanding of the many ways God works to reconcile people to himself, one another, and all creation.

Laypeople read the Jewish scripture and Epistle readings, and a deacon or priest reads the Gospel reading. As the good news for the people of God, the Gospel is often read in the midst of the people. A period of silence for reflection may follow the reading, after which a priest gives a sermon or homily, which is intended to provoke our thoughts about how to apply God's word to our lives and bear witness to that word.

We follow the sermon by affirming our beliefs with the words of the Nicene Creed. We respond to the sermon and to the Nicene Creed by praying for the needs of others, in the Prayers of the People. The Book of Common Prayer presents six forms for the Prayers of the People, which can be modified or replaced entirely. The only requirement is to offer prayers in six areas:

- The Universal Church, its members, and its mission,

- the nation and all in authority,

- the welfare of the world,

- the concerns of the local community,

- those who suffer and those in any trouble, and

- the departed.

During the prayers we also offer our thanksgivings.

The *prayer book* requires that when we come to the Eucharist "we should examine our lives, repent of our sins, and be in love and charity with all people" (Catechism of the Book of Common Prayer, page 860). The sign of reconciliation among people and with God is the exchange of peace. Therefore, before exchanging peace, we confess our sins against God and our neighbor. Because we fail to love God with our whole hearts and continually choose not to love our neighbors as ourselves, we are in need of, and God grants us, mercy and forgiveness regularly.

Forgiveness is healing and renewing, something we need throughout our lives to go forward.

After reestablishing a right relationship with God we exchange the peace. The exchange of peace originates in Jewish practices of being reconciled with one's neighbor before offering a gift to the altar (Matthew 5:23–24). In John 20:19–21, when the risen Jesus appeared to the frightened disciples behind locked doors, he proclaimed, "Peace be with you." It is the peace given to us by the resurrected Christ that we share with one another. The peace ends the Liturgy of the Word.

LITURGY OF THE TABLE

Then he took a loaf of bread, and when he had given thanks, he broke it and gave it to them, saying, "This is my body, which is given for you. Do this in remembrance of me." (Luke 22:19)

The Liturgy of the Table, or Holy Communion, is the climax of our liturgy. It is a response to Jesus' commandment at the Last Supper: we "Do this in remembrance of me." That is, we take, give thanks, break, and give bread in remembrance of Jesus' life on earth, his resurrection, and his coming again in glory. Holy Communion, however, is more than a remembrance. Each Eucharist creates something new. We actively participate in the celebration of Christ's sacrifice, and therefore our lives and actions become part of the offering. We become part of salvation history, which began with creation, continued with the covenant that God offered Abraham and Sarah, and the new covenant in Jesus Christ; it continues today and will be fulfilled at the end of time.

We have six choices for Eucharistic prayers in the Book of Common Prayer: two Rite 1 Eucharistic prayers (I, II) and four Rite 2 Eucharistic prayers (A, B, C, and D). The supplemental text, *Enriching Our Worship 1*, provides three additional Eucharistic prayers. Eucharistic Prayer I was first adopted in 1789. The other prayers expand on this prayer by recounting the stories of creation, the incarnation of Christ, and the coming of Christ.

TAKE, BLESS, BREAK, AND GIVE

Jesus did four important things when he shared a meal with his disciples, and the Liturgy of the Table follows these four actions. Jesus *took bread, blessed it, broke it,* and *gave it.* At the feeding of the five thousand (Matthew 14) Jesus took two loaves of bread and five fish, blessed them, broke them, and gave them to the crowd. It was sufficient to feed more than five thousand. In all three synoptic Gospel accounts of the Last Supper, Jesus performs the same actions — take, bless, break, and give. After the resurrection, Jesus was revealed with these same four actions — take, bless, break, and give — to two followers in the village of Emmaus. The Liturgy of the Table begins with the first action — taking.

Take

We begin with the offertory by gathering gifts from among the people and taking them to the altar, presenting them to God and the church. By presenting our gifts of bread and wine, music, and resources we return the blessing that God gave us — the blessing of creation and our labor. Our labor transforms grapes into wine and wheat into bread. Because God is the giver of all things, ultimately we are *returning* these gifts to God. During the offertory, the deacon or priest

Paten and chalice.

sets the altar table for communion. He or she spreads a white square cloth called the **corporal** on the altar, brings the bread on a plate called a **paten**, and pours the wine and some water into a **chalice**. One chalice is usually placed on the altar, symbolizing that we share one bread and one wine at communion.

Give Thanks

The second main action is to return the blessings, or thank God, for all that God has given us. The **Great Thanksgiving** begins with a dialogue between the celebrant and the people in which we ask God to be present and the people lift their hearts and give thanks to God in the words of the **Sursum Corda** ("Lift up your hearts. *We lift them to the Lord.*") The congregation takes its place among the hosts of heaven and earth to sing praise to God in the **Sanctus** ("Holy, holy, holy Lord . . .").

You can identify the epiclesis visually during the Eucharistic prayers
by noting when the priest raises his or her hands over the bread and the wine.

Our thanksgiving continues by remembering creation and God's saving acts throughout history: the covenant established with Abraham and Sarah and renewed with the people of Israel, the provision of prophets to call us to return, the incarnation, and the life, death, and resurrection of Jesus. We thank God for these mighty works and enduring mercies. This time of remembering continues by recalling the **words of institution** given by Jesus at the Last Supper: "Take, eat: This is my Body which is given for you. Do this in remembrance of me." It is important to remember that this is not a reenactment of the Last Supper, but a prayer to God. The words of institution are addressed not to the congregation, but to God. Following the words of institution, we remember the greatest mystery of our faith with the **memorial acclamation**:

> Christ has died.
> Christ has risen,
> Christ will come again.

In all Episcopal Eucharistic prayers the celebrant asks God to send the Holy Spirit to sanctify the bread and the wine to be the Body and Blood of Jesus Christ. This is called the **epiclesis**. The celebrant has no special powers. In fact, a priest cannot consecrate bread and wine alone. It is through the prayers of all present — lay and ordained ministers alike — and God's blessings that the bread and wine become the body and blood of Christ. We believe that Christ is present in the bread and the wine, and this presence nourishes us and heals us. By partaking in the bread and the wine we are strengthened to serve God in the world.

After the Great Thanksgiving and before the Breaking of the Bread, we say together the Lord's Prayer. The Lord's Prayer reminds us that we are to work to bring God's kingdom to the here and now, that God will provide us nourishment to do so, and that we need to continually ask for forgiveness.

> The bread and the wine are consecrated by the prayers of all the people present. A priest alone cannot consecrate bread and wine.

Break

Following the Great Thanksgiving, the celebrant breaks the bread to distribute it among the people gathered just as Jesus broke the bread to distribute among the disciples. During the breaking of the bread, the congregation sings the **fraction anthem**. The fraction has its name because the word "fraction" means break.

Give

Immediately following the breaking of the bread the people are invited to the altar table to receive both the bread and the wine. In the Episcopal Church all baptized people are welcome to take communion. The congregation comes forward together because we are one people partaking in one body of Christ. Taking communion is also intensely personal. As we eat the bread and drink the wine, we are nourished in a real way by Christ's presence and healing grace in our lives.

Go Out

The final part of Holy Eucharist — the post-communion prayer — proclaims our going out. Unlike all other prayers in the service, this prayer proclaims our readiness to go out into the world to love and to serve. We have been nourished and are ready to do God's work.

Our worship together shapes our prayer. As we come together we are saying who we are: we are God's people. During the Liturgy of the Word we hear about what God has done for us, for all of creation, and we hear how to apply those stories to our lives today. We affirm our faith and pray for others. During the Liturgy of the Table, we remember Christ's death and resurrection and take part in a sacred meal. When we come together to worship each Sunday in these two parts of the liturgy, we continue the work of the earliest members of the church: "They devoted themselves to the apostles' teaching and fellowship, to the breaking of the bread, and the prayers" (Acts 2:42).

PARTICIPANTS IN WORSHIP

All the members of the church participate in worship through song, prayer, giving thanks, and receiving communion. God has created each of us differently, and we each have different gifts to contribute to worship. The table on the next page lists several of the ways the ministers of the church use their gifts to help with worship.

THE CHURCH

Churches are the places within which Christians most often worship together. Because we understand "the church" to be much greater than stone, bricks, and mortar, it seems somewhat odd to define the church merely as a physical place. But that is what most people think of when they hear the word "church." The Catechism tells us, "The Church is the community of the New Covenant." During the Prayers of the People, therefore, when we pray for the church, we pray for the community of baptized. In Form IV, for example, we pray "that all who confess your Name may be united in your truth, live together in your love, and reveal your glory in the world." When we pray for the church we are praying for the baptized members of a living body of Christ who are called to bring God's kingdom to this earth through their presence and actions in the world.

Using the word "church" to mean a community recalls the Greek word *ekklesia* — meaning "called out" — used by the writers of Acts and the Epistles.

Leaders in the Liturgy

Acolyte: A lay minister, often a young person, who helps in a variety of ways, including lighting the candles, carrying the cross and candles in a procession, and assisting in setting the table. Acolytes sometimes wear white albs or white cottas over colored cassocks.

Celebrant (also Presider): The bishop or priest who leads the celebration of the liturgy and presides at the Eucharist and at baptism. Deacons may also serve as celebrants using consecrated elements. During Eucharist, the celebrant says the collect, leads the Great Thanksgiving, and administers the bread at communion. The celebrant generally also reads the Gospel and gives the sermon unless a deacon is present, in which case the deacon reads the Gospel. The celebrant often wears a white alb. Priests wear a stole over both shoulders during the Liturgy of the Word and put a decorated chasuble over the alb during the Liturgy of the Table. Deacons wear a stole over one shoulder.

Choir member: A lay minister who leads sung music during worship. Choirs often sing anthems as musical offerings during the offertory. Choir members often wear robes.

Deacon: If a deacon is present, the deacon should read the Gospel and may lead the Prayers of the People. Deacons also assist at the Table, assist in the administration of the bread and the wine to the people, and dismiss the people. In the absence of a priest, a deacon may distribute Holy Communion from the reserved sacrament.

Eucharistic minister: A lay minister trained in administering the elements. Preference is that a priest or deacon administers the bread and wine during Holy Eucharist.

Reader: A lay minister may read the lessons and lead the Prayers of the People. Deacons may also lead the Prayers of the People. In the Liturgy of the Word, the one who leads the Prayers of the People is called an intercessor.

Verger: A lay minister who assists in the processions of liturgy. The verger is usually robed in a black cassock and carries a verge (staff).

For example, in the letter to the Colossians, Christ is said to be the head of the body, the *ekklesia*, that is, the community of people called out as believers in the risen Christ.

The church is also a physical building — a sacred place Christians have designated for corporate worship. Two Gospels (Luke and John) tell us that until the day of Pentecost the disciples gathered in the room where the risen Christ revealed himself. And as members of the Jewish community, they continued to pray and to teach in the temple. In 70 C.E. the temple was destroyed. Because Christianity was illegal, early followers of the risen Christ met in private homes, often in the upper rooms with a table around which to share a meal. As Christianity grew and spread, members met in houses converted into places of worship or, when persecution was particularly strong, in catacombs, hollowed-out tunnels used for the burial of Jews. The earliest known complete church is a mid-third-century Roman house that was converted into a gathering place for Christians in Dura-Europos (present-day Syria). It included a pool close to the entrance, which was likely used for baptism, and a reception area further inside the house with a table around which the community broke bread. This design is similar to the setup in churches today — a baptismal font near the entrance and a raised sanctuary with an altar for the Liturgy of the Table.

Acolytes often wear cottas over albs.

Unlike the Jewish temple or temples of Greek gods, Christian churches are not seen as a dwelling place for a god, but as a central meeting place. Many churches today follow the basic design of the fourth-century civic basilica — a rectangular building with a curved apse for a throne at which a magistrate or military governor could hear civil cases of dispute. The reason the churches took on this style is that the civic basilica was the standard gathering place when the emperor Constantine legalized Christianity. We can trace much of our church furnishings to the early church and to the secular buildings of the fourth century.

The diagram at the top of the following page shows the layout of a typical Episcopal church today. The overall shape is a Latin cross, or cruciform, which developed when Gothic architects added two rooms — one for the priests and another for the remains of the dead — on either side of the long nave and circular apse of the Roman basilica. The cruciform is comprised of three main areas: the nave, the transept, and the chancel. The **chancel** contains the sanctuary, pulpit, lectern, and altar. It may end at the apse and is often raised

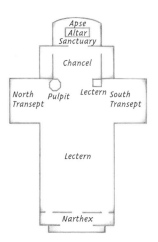

Cruciform church.

in elevation and separated from the nave by a rail or screen. The **altar**, which rests within the sanctuary, is the table around which Holy Communion is celebrated. The altar represents the presence of God and is the focus of our worship. Therefore, it is situated at the head of the cross, which is generally oriented so that the congregation faces the east — the direction of the rising sun, a symbol of the resurrected Christ. The two areas created by the **transept** typically house chapels for more intimate prayer and worship. The **nave** is where worshipers gather to hear the Word and participate in the consecration of the bread and wine of communion.

The word "nave" comes from the Latin word *navis*, meaning ship. A ship is an early symbol of the church.

Because baptism is the rite through which one becomes a member of the church, a **baptismal font** or pool is usually close to the entrance of the church. This grand design emphasizes the transcendence and mystery of God and reflects a class structure of society. St. John the Divine in New York City (*www.stjohndivine.org*) and our National Cathedral in Washington, D.C. (*www.cathedral.org*) are cruciform-style cathedrals.

Another design is illustrated here. In this circular layout, the altar is more clearly the central element around which people gather. This simple design returns to the layout of the synagogues and the temple familiar to Jesus and is likely closer to the worship spaces of early Christians than the cruciform layout. This design emphasizes the participation of all members in the liturgy. St. Gregory's in San Francisco (*www.saintgregorys.org*) is built in a circular pattern.

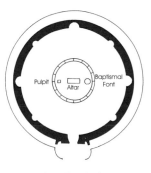

Circular church design.

Regardless of the specific design of your particular church, the furnishings are meant to facilitate and unify the two main parts of the Holy Eucharist: the Liturgy of the Word and the Liturgy of the Table. The Liturgy of the Word takes place nearer to the people. The Jewish scripture and Epistle readings are generally read from the lectern on the Epistle side of the sanctuary while the Gospel is read either among the people or from the Gospel lectern, or pulpit. The Liturgy of the Table moves the central action toward the altar table, where the bread and wine are consecrated and received by those worshiping together.

People have been building sacred places for worship of God since ancient times. Remember, Abraham and Sarah created stone altars to worship at the roadside. The Israelites built a tabernacle so God would dwell with them. The Hebrews built the temple at Jerusalem. Muslims have mosques, and Jews have temples. Christians have churches. We also worship in places other than church — around the evening supper table when we say grace together, on a mountaintop when we thank God for God's beautiful creation, and when we set aside time in a quiet place in our homes to pray and meditate on God's word.

We can even worship in cyberspace. At *geraniumfarm.org*, for example, you can light a candle and offer a prayer, and you can say the Daily Office at *www.dailyoffice.org*.

SYMBOLS OF WORSHIP

Have you ever smelled fresh-baked bread or pie at home? Your mouth begins to water. You turn the corner into the kitchen almost expecting to see your family gathered around the table as they have done many times before. In that one smell many memories of grace are piled up and brought into the present. And it calls out a response of gratitude. Worship is similar. We enter a church to see familiar symbols of Jesus and God's never-ending love. Jesus, the good shepherd, in a stained-glass window. A vine with grapes reminding us of Jesus, the true vine. The cross reminding us of Jesus' death and resurrection. We may smell the lingering scent of incense. Through our senses we know the presence of God — the many moments of prayer and worship offered to us, begging from our whole being a response of love and thanksgiving.

Throughout the liturgy our senses are stimulated. We see the cross processed with candles to the altar, we listen to the word of God, we proclaim God's praises, we exchange the peace with our hands, we smell the scent of incense, and we eat and drink at the table. By using all our senses we are

---

Vestments

A **stole** is worn by bishops and priests over both shoulders and by a deacon over the left shoulder.

An **alb** is a white garment worn by bishops, priests, deacons, and acolytes during the entire liturgy.

A **chasuble** is a long sleeveless garment worn over the alb during the Liturgy of the Table. When laid out flat it is generally oval with a hole in the middle for the celebrant's head. Chasubles vary in color based on the church season.

A **miter** is a tall pointed hat worn by the bishop.

A **crosier** is a pastoral staff that symbolizes the pastoral ministry of the bishop. A bishop generally holds the crosier during the reading of the Gospel, while walking into and out of the service, and during the absolution and blessing. It is a sign of authority.

---

reminded that Christ is alive with us today, guiding us and nourishing us. And such rich worship is the right response to the first commandment: to love God with all our heart, with all our soul, and with all our mind, and with all our strength. These sights, sounds, and smells are symbols of our faith. Each symbol is rich with meaning and experience, pointing beyond itself to God's actions in the world throughout history. To understand the power of a symbol, think about the cross. It symbolizes the suffering of dying on the cross as well as the joy of the resurrected Christ. For some it represents comfort in times of trouble and for others Jesus' conquering of death and dominion in the world. The cross carries all these meanings.

VESTMENTS

It is common in the Episcopal Church for leaders of the liturgy to wear special clothing called **vestments**. Holy Eucharist is a celebration, and celebrations often call for special garments. Vestments express both the solemnity

The celebrant wears a poncho-like garment called a chasuble over a white alb along with a long narrow piece of fabric called a stole placed over the shoulders.

and joy of worship. Because special vestments are reserved for particular participants, vestments become symbols. The **stole,** a long strip of cloth worn by a priest or bishop over both shoulders or by a deacon over one shoulder and to the side, for example, is a symbol of their ordination. The Book of Common Prayer does not require the use of particular vestments, but allows for the variety of customs of the local community. You can see a beautiful display of colors and customs by attending various churches throughout the year or at the National Acolyte Festival at the National Cathedral in Washington, D.C., in October. Still, some customs are shared by all Episcopalians. The stole is one.

THE CHURCH YEAR

Then God said, "Let there be Light"; and there was light. And God saw that the light was good; and God separated the light from the darkness. God called the light Day, and the darkness he called Night. (Genesis 1:3–5)

From very beginning of creation, God is the ruler of all things, including time and space. And God has redeemed God's people throughout time — not just long ago but also today. So we claim this redemption as a present reality by marking history with the church year. The calendar wheel illustrates the church year. The year is anchored by two feasts: Christmas Day and Easter. These two feast days determine the dates of the seven seasons of the year. Christmas is always December 25 while Easter Day is the first Sunday after the first full moon after the vernal equinox (March 21). As you follow the wheel clockwise beginning with Advent, you can see that the year is divided into Advent, Christmas, Epiphany, Lent, Easter, Pentecost, and the Season after Pentecost. Each season is associated with a color that we use in church vestments, altar cloths, and banners. Colors are visual reminders, and symbols, of each season.

We begin the year with **Advent** in expectation of Christ's coming into the world and Christ's return. Advent, which means "coming," begins four Sundays before Christmas Day. The color for Advent is either blue for hope of the peace that Christ brings or purple or linen for penitence in preparation for welcoming God's entrance into this world as the Christ child. **Christmas** begins on Christmas Day and ends twelve days later on January 6, Epiphany. During Christmas we recall the stories of Christ's birth. Because Christmas is a time of celebration, its color is either white for purity or gold.

Epiphany means "to show forth." On the Feast of Epiphany we celebrate the visit of the Magi to the Christ child. On the first Sunday after the Feast of Epiphany we celebrate the baptism of Christ. The color of the Feast of Epiphany is white. All other days in Epiphany are green, which symbolizes life and growth. Epiphany ends on Ash Wednesday, the first day of Lent. **Lent** is a time of prayer, fasting, and penitence in preparation for Easter. The early church used this time to finalize the training of new believers, preparing them for initiation into the church through baptism at the Great Vigil of Easter. The Great Vigil of Easter today is also a preferred time of baptism. During Lent we renew our commitment to Christ and resolve to take on the difficult task of living as Christians in this world. Lent lasts forty days, beginning on Ash Wednesday and ending with Holy Week. If you count those days, you'll find that there are forty-six days. The five Sundays in Lent and Palm Sunday are not counted because they celebrate Christ's resurrection. The color of Lent is purple or linen and the color of Holy Week is red.

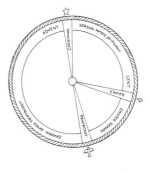

Calendar wheel.

The traditional colors for the seasons of the church year are:

Advent – blue, purple, or linen
Christmas – white or gold
Season after Epiphany – green
Lent – purple or linen
Easter – white
Pentecost – red
Season after Pentecost – green

Three days in Holy Week, called the **Paschal Triduum** (Latin for "three days of Easter"), are the most sacred days of the church year. The Paschal Triduum begins with the Maundy Thursday service in the evening, continues with Good Friday, and peaks with the Great Easter Vigil on Saturday night. On Maundy Thursday we remember three actions of Jesus: washing the feet of the disciples, instituting the sacrament of the Eucharist, and giving the new commandment, "to love one another as I have loved you." This service precedes the darkest day of the year: Good Friday, the day we commemorate Christ's death on the cross.

Good Friday is an essential part of our celebration of Easter. Without death, Christ has not conquered death. The Great Easter Vigil begins after sundown on Holy Saturday and before sunrise on Easter Sunday. It is the first service of Easter Day. During this service we light the Paschal Candle to represent the light of the living Christ in our world, hear the record of God's saving deeds in history, baptize new members, and administer the Easter communion. The Easter Vigil begins in solemnity and ends with triumph.

We celebrate **Easter** for fifty days, beginning on Easter Sunday and ending with Pentecost Sunday. Because Easter is a season of triumph, its color is white. The fortieth day of Easter is Ascension Day, the day we commemorate Christ's ascension into heaven. The final day of Easter is the Feast of Pentecost. On this day we celebrate the day the Holy Spirit came from heaven as tongues of fire and rested on the twelve apostles and celebrate the beginning of the church. The color of the Feast of Pentecost is red, representing fire and symbolizing love and zeal.

The Sundays after Pentecost and before Advent are called the **Season after Pentecost**. It is the longest season of the church year, lasting twenty-two to twenty-seven Sundays. This is a time for growing our faith and doing the work of ministry, emphasized by its liturgical color, green.

✝ TRANSFORMING QUESTIONS

1. **Be Attentive:** Recall a recent experience in corporate worship. What did you notice? Include all your senses. Write words that you recall from hymns, prayers, and readings. What experiences from your week did you bring with you to worship? What were you thinking and feeling at the time?

2. **Be Intelligent:** What does your experience of worship mean?

3. **Be Reasonable:** The introduction to this chapter talked about Annie Dillard's description of worship as an event that requires crash helmets. What might this say about your experience? Take a second look at what you remember. What new insights does your reflection on your experience offer?

4. **Be Responsible:** Does your worship experience suggest a response in your daily life? What might that be?

5. **Be in Love Transformed:** The next time you prepare for worship, be ready to meet the Holy Spirit. Is there something in the experience you described that is nudging you to act differently to be in that "thin place" of worship?

Chapter Ten

Sacraments

CALLED TO BE...IN LOVE

A quiet reformation in religious education began within the Roman Catholic Church in the 1950s, took hold during the 1960s, and continues to unfold in many churches. As I experienced it while serving as a Roman Catholic priest from 1963 to 1981, it expressed theologically the relationship between sacraments and commandments, between grace and law. Theology always wins, no matter how distant one might think theology is from real life.

It was once common to think about religion first as commandments and law, that is, what I must do; then about sacraments and grace, that is, my relationship with God. It may not have been your experience, but it was mine.

This priority of commandments suggested that religion was about morality, about keeping the law. God's help was accessed in sacraments which, so perceived, were received rather than celebrated. It was the practical expression of misinformed theology, namely: I act first. God responds.

Sacraments are "so what" encounters with divinity. Okay, I've been baptized. So what?

Recognize who you are, in Love. What you are to do and how you are to live follow upon your God-given relationship as a new creation in the sacramental encounter with divinity. God takes the initiative. God loves you, before you even think about God, in fact, despite what you think about God. Sacraments are interpersonal acts of love, God inviting us to be...in Love.

Early Christian thinkers spoke about sacraments with two words that played against each other, one Greek and one Latin, to describe partially veiled and partially unveiled encounters with divinity. Greek teachers used *musterion,* from which we derive "mystery," to emphasize what was hidden, beyond us, in the encounter. Latin teachers translated the Greek word as *sacramentum,* that is, sign, sacrament, to suggest something visible in the encounter. The sacraments of the church, thus, are visible realities that suggest the hidden presence of God.

168

Because you have been invited by God, through the sacraments of the church, to be...in Love, your mission as a Christian is to live God's love, to tell by how you live what you have seen and heard...in Love.

Religion continues as a response to this wonderful mystery in which we are changed. Religion continues as spirituality, celebration, thanksgiving, ministry, lifestyle, stewardship—neither law nor duty nor morality nor ethics, but a free and loving response to the freely given love of God.

At the same time, however, we know that faith communities and those of us within them are called to the impossible. "If you're going to be Christian," Jesuit activist Dan Berrigan has said, "you'd better look good on wood."

Writer and philosopher Nikos Kazantzakis writes of his conversation with a saintly monk. "Father Makarios, do you still wrestle with the devil?"

"Not any longer," said the monk. "I have grown old and he has grown old with me. He doesn't have the strength. I wrestle with God."

"With God? And you hope to win?"

"I hope to lose," Father Makarios said.

The temptation story of Jesus, in Luke, comes right after his baptism. He hears God's call, "You are my son, the beloved; with you I am well pleased," with its suffering servant undertone from Isaiah. A Jew who was familiar with his scriptures might respond to those words with Tevye in *Fiddler on the Roof*: "If this is how you treat your chosen friends, God, no wonder you have so few."

"Allow me to suggest Plan B, a miracle, magic, smoke and mirrors," the devil said as Jesus "was led by the Spirit in the wilderness" to wrestle with God about what it might mean to be God's beloved. He recognized the lie he heard in the desert.

Going, then, to his hometown synagogue, he owned God's call. He read from Isaiah: "The Spirit of the Lord is upon me. He has anointed me to bring good news to the poor,...to proclaim release to the captives, recovery of sight to the blind, to let the oppressed go free....Today, this scripture has been fulfilled in your hearing." His life was based on a true story. He told it anew, putting himself in it.

When you wrestle with God about good inspirations you may have been resisting, one of two things can happen. Winning isn't one. Either you walk away from the relationship, or you wrestle until you lose. When God wins, you have reason to celebrate.

God calls churches, faith communities, to preview on earth as in heaven the already-but-not-yet reality of God's kingdom. To live as though the kingdom has come, in the reality of the already-but-not-yet right relationships of the kingdom. When you celebrate a sacrament and consider "so what," think of the biblical notion, kingdom of God, with Verna Dozier's paraphrase, the dream of God.   **—B.L.**

◆   ◆   ◆

THE SACRAMENTS

Sacraments are "outward and visible signs of inward and spiritual grace, given by Christ as sure and certain means by which we receive that grace." The Episcopal Church recognizes two great sacraments of the Bible (baptism and Eucharist) and five sacramental rites (confirmation, ordination, holy matrimony, reconciliation of the penitent, and unction of the sick). In Christ, God came to dwell among us. Through the Holy Spirit, God and Christ continue to dwell with us. In the sacraments we recognize God's active presence in our lives.

Each sacrament has something visible or sensibly perceptible. We can see the water poured in baptism, the laying on of hands at confirmation and ordination, the rings exchanged at marriage, the bread and wine for the Eucharist, and the oil at healing. We can see, feel, smell, taste, and touch them.

> God is "the one in whom we live and move and have our being" (Acts 17:28). Because we are physical beings God is revealed to us by our senses. Sacraments reflect that reality.

Be attentive to how God calls you to be in Love. What does that mean for your life? How do God's invitations to you to be in Love relate to the sacraments of the church? How might you respond again and again and again?

Outward Visible Sign

The signs and gestures of the sacraments are living symbols that God, Jesus Christ, and the Holy Spirit are alive in our human experiences, transforming us into the image and likeness of God. For each sacrament, an external sign symbolizes an internal transformation of the human spirit by grace. The water of baptism signifies dying and rebirth, eating and drinking symbolizes refreshment and restoration, the laying on of hands signifies the power of the Holy Spirit, a ring signifies union, and oil signifies strengthening or healing. Through the sacraments Christ enters our lives and continues God's work of redemption. God is with us here and now, in our lives today and every day in very real and tangible ways.

THE SEVEN SACRAMENTS		
	Outward Visible Sign	**Inward Spiritual Grace**
Baptism	water	• death to sin • birth into God's family
Eucharist	bread and wine	• body and blood of Christ • forgiveness of sins • strengthening of our union with Christ and one another • foretaste of heavenly banquet
Confirmation	laying on of hands by a bishop	• strengthening of the Holy Spirit
Marriage	exchange of rings and vows	• love of Christ for the church
Reconciliation of a penitent	absolution by a priest	• forgiveness of sins • strength for right living
Unction	oil and/or laying on of hands	• healing of mind, body, and spirit
Ordination	laying on of hands by a bishop for a priest and deacon and by three bishops for consecration of a bishop	• authority and grace of the Holy Spirit

Inward Spiritual Grace

It is important to understand that the power of the sacraments comes from God. Grace is not something that we can earn or achieve. It is freely and abundantly given by God to all people. The effect of grace is not based on the personal faith or moral character of the person administering a sacrament nor the faith of the person receiving the sacrament, but on the power of the Holy Spirit.

Our Response

The rainbow is a sign of God's covenant. Throughout the Jewish scriptures God reminds us, "You will be my people, and I will be your God." The covenant is a relationship. God will provide for his people. And with God's gift of free choice we can choose to respond to God by orienting our heart and mind toward receiving God's transforming grace. At baptism we turn away from evil and accept Jesus Christ. Before Eucharist we examine our lives, repent of our sins, and restore right relationships with others. In each sacrament we respond to God's love. God showers grace upon everyone, but like the seed that falls on rocky ground or fertile soil, our response can either keep that seed from taking root or it can nurture that seed of grace to bear fruit.

BAPTISM

Do you not know that all of us who have been baptized into Christ Jesus were baptized into his death? Therefore we have been buried with him by baptism into death, so that, just as Christ was raised from the dead by the glory of the Father, so we too might walk in newness of life. (Romans 6:3–4)

We baptize in the Name of the Father, and of the Son, and of the Holy Spirit. **Baptism** is full initiation by water and the Holy Spirit into the body of Christ and the church. Through baptism God adopts us into God's family and makes us members of Christ's body, the church. As such, it is a necessary sacrament for all Christians and is the foundation for all participation and ministry in the church.

Outward and Visible Sign

The water of baptism is rich with history and symbolism. God breathed over the waters at creation. God led Israel through the Red Sea into the Promised Land. In water Jesus was baptized by John and anointed by the Holy Spirit. The water with which we baptize is this very same water of liberation and rebirth.

Inward and Spiritual Grace

By our baptism we share in this rich history of restoration. As Paul told the Romans in the scriptural passage beginning this section, at baptism our old selves die. Our sins are washed away. We are buried with Christ in his death, and we also share in his resurrection. Just as we burst into this world through the waters of the womb, we come out of the waters of baptism a new creation. We are reborn into God's family and marked as Christ's own forever. Through baptism, like ancient Israel we all share the promise of God's kingdom. In baptism we are brought into the fellowship of believers, forever changing

A dove symbolizing the Holy Spirit hovering over a pedestal font.

our selves and our community. The inward and spiritual grace is fourfold: union with Christ, birth into God's family, forgiveness of sins, and new life in the Holy Spirit.

 If sacraments are "so what" encounters with divinity, what's the "so what" of baptism?

Baptism is full initiation into the body of Christ. Nothing can take our membership away. In baptism we are sealed by the Holy Spirit and marked as Christ's own *forever.*

How Do We Respond?

In the early church, adults preparing for baptism, called **catechumens**, studied for two or three years before being baptized. Catechumens were allowed to attend Christian services, but only the Liturgy of the Word. The unbaptized had to leave before the Eucharist. When their lives conformed to the teachings of Christ and their faith was strong, they were baptized. Only after baptism were they fully welcomed to participate in the holy mysteries — that is, Eucharist. Being a Christian in the early centuries of the first millennium is much different than today. The world was hostile toward Christians. And to be a Christian might have meant giving up one's livelihood in order to live rightly. Years of preparation provided the knowledge and strength needed to persevere in the life of a Christian.

Today, in the liturgy of baptism candidates begin with two main actions: to turn *away* from evil (renounce Satan) and then to turn *toward* Jesus Christ (accept Jesus as their Savior). In ancient liturgies, candidates faced the west (the setting sun) to renounce Satan and physically turned toward the east (the rising sun) to profess their faith in God. In the Service of Holy Baptism, candidates make a threefold renunciation of Satan and threefold profession of faith. In the case of infant baptism, these actions and promises are made by godparents on behalf of the baptized.

During the baptismal rite, the congregation promises to support the newly baptized in their life in Christ. Baptism transforms not just the one being baptized, but the whole body of Christ — every member of the church. To-gether with the candidate, the community renews the baptismal covenant: professing a faith in God the Father, Jesus Christ, the Son of God, and God the Holy Spirit and promising to continue to live a life in Christ.

EUCHARIST

When the hour came, he took his place at the table, and the apostles with him. He said to them, "I have eagerly desired to eat this Passover with you before I suffer; for I tell you, I will not eat it until it is fulfilled in the kingdom of God." Then he took a cup, and after giving thanks he said, "Take this and divide it among yourselves; for I tell you that from now on I will not drink of the fruit of the vine until the kingdom of God comes." Then he took a loaf of bread, and when he had given thanks, he broke it and gave it to them, saying, "This is my body, which is given for you. Do this in remembrance of me." And he did the same with the cup after supper, saying, "This cup that is poured out for you is the new covenant in my blood." (Luke 22:14–20)

The elements of Eucharist — bread and wine.

During the Last Supper, Jesus instituted these words, "Do this in remembrance of me." Jesus took the bread and the wine, gave thanks, and gave it to them. "This is my body, which is given for you." The bread and the wine are the outward and visible signs of the inward and spiritual grace of the Body and Blood of Christ.

According to Anglican belief, Christ's body and blood are truly present in the consecrated bread and wine. This doctrine is called **Real Presence**. According to this belief, knowing how Christ is present in the sacraments is not central. What is central is the belief that by eating the bread and the wine recipients are united in communion with Christ. This doctrine contrasts with **transubstantiation,** which is the belief that when consecrated, the substance of the bread and the wine are transformed into the substance of Christ's body and blood, while the appearance as bread and wine continues to be unchanged. The Episcopal Church embraces a theology of Real Presence.

You can hear the doctrine of Real Presence in the words of Eucharistic Prayer A:

> *Sanctify them by your Holy Spirit to be for your people the Body and Blood of your Son, the holy food and drink of new and unending life in him.*

The celebrant asks that Christ be present for the people.

The Purpose of Holy Eucharist

Through the celebration of Holy Eucharist we remember Jesus' life, death, and resurrection and await Christ's coming again in glory. We understand the celebration of Eucharist as a **memorial**, not as a reenactment of a past event of the Last Supper, but as the acclamation of a present reality of Christ among us, a living sacrifice, for us today. God's saving acts throughout history and the future reality of our union with all creation are made present to us in the Eucharist.

Having been invited, through the Eucharist, to be in Love transformed, how do you live God's love?

A way to understand what we mean by memorial is by looking at the word "anamnesis." **Anamnesis** is an active form of memory that connects the past to the present in a way that allows us to become a present participant in the past event. Have you ever smelled perfume that reminded you so strongly of a person that you could almost hear her voice speaking to you or hear the pattern of her footsteps nearby? You look around, feeling her presence as if she were with you. That is anamnesis: a remembrance of a past event in a way that it becomes present to you today.

In the Eucharist the past events that become present to you are God's saving actions throughout history — at creation, in the covenant made with Israel, and most of all sending his only son to dwell among us, allowing him to die on the cross and raising him up in resurrection. Not only are past events made present to us; so are future events of the heavenly banquet — when we become fully one with God. All time collapses in one moment in which we can partake in all of salvation history — past, present, and future. Through the Eucharist we are forgiven of our past sins, strengthened in our current union with Christ, and given a foretaste of heaven.

How Do We Prepare?

Holy Eucharist is a necessary part of a life in Christ. Because by our nature we are separated from God, we continually fall into sin and are in need of forgiveness and healing of our brokenness. Through Holy Communion we are forgiven and our union with Christ is made strong. We come before Christ willingly. We yearn to be in right relationship with all people. Therefore, before the Eucharist we examine our lives to see where we have fallen short, we repent of our sins, and we extend our love and charity to all people.

The Liturgy of the Word prepares us in this very way. Except during the Season of Easter, together the congregation says the Confession of Sin. We confess that we have done what we ought not to and not done what we ought to and ask for mercy so that we may reestablish a right relationship with God and others. After the priest pronounces God's forgiveness with an absolution we demonstrate that we are in love and charity with others by exchanging the peace. After the peace Holy Communion begins.

CONFIRMATION

When he came to Nazareth, where he had been brought up, he went to the synagogue on the Sabbath day, as was his custom. He stood up to read, and the scroll of the prophet Isaiah was given to him. He unrolled the scroll and found the place where it was written:

> *The Spirit of the Lord is upon me,*
> *because he has anointed me*
> *to bring good news to the poor.*
> *He has sent me to proclaim release to the captives*
> *and recovery of sight to the blind,*
> *to let the oppressed go free,*
> *to proclaim the year of the Lord's favor.*

And he rolled up the scroll, gave it back to the attendant, and sat down. The eyes of all in the synagogue were fixed on him. Then he began to say to them, "Today this scripture has been fulfilled in your hearing." All spoke well of him and were amazed at the gracious words that came from his mouth. They said, "Is not this Joseph's son?" (Luke 4:14–22)

The passage above depicts Jesus telling his hometown that he has been called to serve. This passage also illustrates how Jesus grew in stature: from a baby presented to God in the temple when he was eight days old to a young man reading in the synagogue and proclaiming his purpose as God's son. The elders were amazed, remembering that this was Joseph's son. Jesus had grown in stature and into his public ministry.

At baptism we are reborn, like infants, to a new family of God. As we continue in life, like Jesus, we grow in stature within the community. Through experience and learning we gain knowledge of Christ, ourselves, our call, and our community. Through practice, we exercise and strengthen our gifts for ministry.

At some point as we mature into adult-hood, we are expected to affirm our faith pro-claimed at baptism and renew our baptismal promises as God's call to us. Confirmation is the rite in which we do this. **Confirmation** is the rite in which we make a mature commitment to Christ and receive continu-ing strength from the Holy Spirit. During the Rite of Confirmation we reaffirm our renun-ciation of evil and renew our commitment to Jesus Christ. Just as with baptism, the con-gregation promises to do all in its power to support the candidates in their life in Christ. The bishop then leads the candidates and the congregation in renewing the Baptismal Covenant.

At confirmation we receive continuing strength by the Holy Spirit.

Outward and Visible Sign and Inward and Spiritual Grace

Once the Baptismal Covenant is renewed, the bishop lays his or her hands on the candidate, asking God to strengthen the candidate and empower him or her for service. Jesus laid his hands on those whom he healed and blessed many times throughout his ministry. This physical contact powerfully illustrates the granting of power to the one being blessed. The bishop also prays, asking God to give the candidate strength of the Holy Spirit, power for service, and sustenance for continued life in Christ.

How Does a Candidate Prepare?

Candidates for confirmation are baptized members of the body of Christ. Because confirmation is a mature commitment, candidates prepare by learning about Christian faith: what Christians believe and what it means to follow Christ. Candidates must also repent of their sins and be ready to confess Jesus Christ as their Lord and Savior.

 The outward sign of confirmation is laying on of hands; the inward grace is strengthening by the Holy Spirit.

It is important to remember that those who are baptized are *full* members of the body of Christ. Confirmation does not complete initiation, nor is confirmation necessary to receive communion. Confirmation is an opportunity for those who are baptized to make a mature and independent affirmation of faith and for the bishop to confirm the blessing of the church.

MARRIAGE

For you were called to freedom, brothers and sisters; only do not use your freedom as an opportunity for self-indulgence, but through love become slaves to one another. For the whole law is summed up in a single commandment, "You shall love your neighbor as yourself." (Galatians 5:13–14)

All people are called to faithful relationships with others. Some are called to Holy Matrimony. **Holy Matrimony** is the physical and spiritual binding together of two people before God and his people for mutual joy, and with the intention of a lifelong commitment. After taking one another in matrimony, the couple exchange rings as signs of the vows by which they bind themselves to each other.

 The outward sign of marriage is the exchange of rings and vows; the inward grace is the love of Christ for the church.

A Covenant Relationship

Marriage is a covenant, a binding agreement that is freely entered into by two people. In marriage, two people bind themselves to one another in the presence of God. As a covenant, marriage mirrors God's relationship with his chosen people and Christ's relationship to the church.

As we have discussed before, our relationship with God is a covenant relationship. God initiated a covenant with the Hebrews in which he promised to be their God and they would be his people. The people were required to "be faithful; to love justice, do mercy, and walk humbly with their God" (Book of Common Prayer, page 847). God initiated a New Covenant through Christ, granting us salvation and requiring that we believe in Christ and keep his commandments. In both the New Covenant and the Old Covenant, God makes promises and the people are required, but not forced, to respond. The covenant requires a response, an action by all those entering it.

Preparation for Marriage and the Grace of God

Those who marry come to know deeply the scripture passage that begins this section. A married couple are two people serving one another in freedom and fulfilling the central commandment to love your neighbor as yourself. They have promised to love, comfort, honor, and keep, and, forsaking all others, be faithful to one another. They have promised to love and serve one another in all circumstances of life. Every couple faces trying situations some time during their marriage. The couple may argue, but they have promised to love one another. One may become ill and require great assistance to regain health, but each has promised to honor and keep the other in times of sickness. One person may meet someone else who may also seem like a compatible partner, but the married couple has promised to forsake all others.

IHS, the traditional monogram for Jesus, holds together two interlocked wedding bands.

God has bound the couple together and has given them abundant grace and power to keep their promises. During the marriage ceremony, the priest asks for God's blessing and assistance to keep the couple's promises of fidelity and steadfast love. In a public ceremony, the Christian community also promises to uphold the couple in their marriage.

Procreation and Sexual Intimacy

Marriage is a gift from God for mutual joy and companionship. When it is God's will, marriage is also for the procreation of children and their nurture. We add "when it is God's will" because not all couples bear children. The sacrament of marriage grants grace to a couple and to a community, regardless of a purpose beyond two people making a lifelong commitment to one another in love and with the Holy Spirit.

Sexual intimacy is part of God's creation and strengthens the union of two people. It draws together two people committed in marriage into communion of body and soul, further binding the two into mutual companionship and strengthening their life together. Sexual intimacy is one way a married couple expresses their deep and abiding love for one another. The depth of intimacy shared by sexual intercourse leaves the lasting mark of each person's body and soul on the other.

RECONCILIATION OF A PENITENT

Jesus said to them again, "Peace be with you. As the Father has sent me, so I send you." When he had said this, he breathed on them and said to them, "Receive the Holy Spirit. If you forgive the sins of any, they are forgiven them; if you retain the sins of any, they are retained." (John 20:21–23)

"Peace be with you." These are the first words that the risen Christ said to the disciples. Jesus would have used the Hebrew word *shalom*, which has a broad meaning that includes wholeness, health, prosperity, and right relationships. Peace is Christ's gift to the world. Jesus' next words give the disciples the authority to offer God's forgiveness to others. This was how the disciples were to restore wholeness to the body of Christ: to forgive.

Symbol for reconciliation created by Episcopal artist Jan Neal.

God yearns for our return. And our own inclination to ask for pardon stems from God's yearning. We practice confession and receive forgiveness regularly in our worship together. On Sundays we confess that we have not loved God with our whole heart and have not loved our neighbor as ourselves. We name the ways we have fallen short of God's desires for us. The priest expresses God's forgiveness. As a people reconciled to one another, we then share the peace — the peace that Christ offered the disciples.

We may also confess our sins in the sacrament of reconciliation. **Reconciliation of a Penitent** is "the rite by which those who repent confess their sins to a priest and receive the assurances of pardon and the grace of absolution" (Book of Common Prayer, page 861). The outward and visible sign of reconciliation is the laying on of hands. The inward and spiritual grace is restoration of a right relationship with God and the body of Christ.

Sin

To understand the need for repentance and reconciliation, let's first discuss what sin is. We do not always live into God's will for us. Many times we don't even *listen* for what God desires of us. Our own desires and egos get in the way so that our choices do not conform to God's will. The Hebrew word for sin, *het*, translated literally means "miss the mark." When we sin we fail to live up to the image of God in which we were created; we miss the mark of what God intends for us.

The Catechism defines sin as "seeking our own will instead of the will of God, thus distorting our relationship with God, with other people, and with all creation" (Book of Common Prayer, page 848). The Ten Commandments explicitly state our duty to God and our neighbors. Actions contrary to these commandments distort our relationship with God and others.

Jesus gave us the two commandments upon which hang all the law and the prophets: "You shall love the Lord your God with all your heart, and with all your soul, and with all your mind," and "You shall love your neighbor as yourself." These two commandments provide the basis for examining our lives and discerning when we have missed the mark. When have you not loved God? When have you not loved yourself? When have you not loved your neighbor?

Repenting: Changing Direction

God yearns for our pardon and peace. God sent Jesus to bear our sins on the cross and reconcile us to God. And the risen Christ proclaimed God's desire to the disciples with his greeting of "peace." We are called to repent as a regular part of our worship together. Morning Prayer, Evening Prayer, and Holy Eucharist all include the call to repent, an opportunity for a general confession, and a general absolution. God continually offers healing grace and pardon. It is our response to examine our lives, repent of our sins, and set firm our resolve to make amends.

The sacrament of reconciliation helps in the process of changing our hearts and the direction of our lives toward God's will. It is not a necessary rite, but is offered to all people. For some a general absolution does not meet their needs. They may need help and counsel to make amends. They may have committed a grave offense for which they doubt they may be pardoned. They may need the strength of the church to face their sins. The sacrament of reconciliation provides the benefit of absolution, the assurance of pardon, spiritual counsel, and advice, and the strengthening of faith.

Preparation for Reconciliation

God's forgiving grace is offered to us always, abundantly, even *before* we have turned away from God. God pardons us freely; pardon is not earned. It is we who are responding to God's forgiveness in advance by recognizing our need to change. God's grace is the source of our repentance. Our desire to repent is a response to God's forgiveness. We prepare for the Rite of Reconciliation by:

1. examining our actions and inactions for unfaithfulness.

2. expressing our regret and sorrow.

3. setting our resolve to conform to God's will.

In each of these, we acknowledge our complete reliance on the grace of God alone. We need God to know where we have missed the mark. It is through God's yearning for wholeness that we feel regret and sorrow. It is with God's strength that we work to conform to God's will.

The Rite of Reconciliation

The service has two forms. Here, we review form one. The Rite of Reconciliation can be anywhere. Wherever two meet in Christ's name, Christ will be present. But, generally, the penitent and the priest meet face-to-face in the priest's office or study, or in the church.

> The gospel tells us that the impulse to repent and the desire for forgiveness spring from God's prior longing for our reconciliation.   —Martin L. Smith, S.S.J.E.[22]

The penitent begins by requesting a blessing. Doing so shows that we need God's help for self-examination and confession. God's grace is the source of our desire to repent. The penitent continues by confessing to God and the church his or her offenses, expressing a resolve to amend sinful ways, and asking for God's forgiveness. The priest serves as a witness to the confession. After the confession, the priest responds by offering counsel and advice. The priest then lays hands on the penitent and pronounces absolution. The penitent thanks God. The priest concludes with a dismissal and a request for prayer. This final request reminds us that the penitent and priest stand together in need of God's mercy.

---

22. Martin L. Smith, S.S.J.E., *Reconciliation* (Cambridge, Mass.: Cowley Publications, 1985), 2.

Role of the Priest. We confess to and receive absolution by a priest for a variety of reasons. Those serving as priests are recognized as having the gifts of wisdom and counsel necessary for wise advice. But more importantly we can be pardoned only by those whom we have offended. Since sins are an offense to God, only God can pardon. God gave Jesus the authority to forgive sins, and Jesus gave that authority to the apostles. Through the laying on of hands during ordination, this authority is also given to priests. Priests therefore have the authority to proclaim God's pardon on God's behalf. A second reason we confess to a priest is that sins weaken relationships in the entire community. Because a priest represents the body of Christ, a priest can grant us pardon on behalf of the community. Through reconciliation our relationship with God, others, and creation is made right.

Confidentiality. Confession is always confidential. A priest cannot reveal the contents of a confession to anyone. Civil law in the United States honors this confidentiality so that even in a court of law a priest cannot be made to tell what is said in confession. This provides the penitent the security of complete silence. The sins revealed are held in God's loving embrace and the silence of the church.

HEALING OF THE SICK

Are any among you sick? They should call for the elders of the church and have them pray over them, anointing them with oil in the name of the Lord. The prayer of faith will save the sick, and the Lord will raise them up; and anyone who has committed sins will be forgiven. (James 4:14–15)

This passage from James tells us that the purpose of healing is twofold: to raise up the sick and to forgive their sins. **Healing of the Sick** is "the rite of anointing the sick with oil, or the laying on of hands, by which God's grace is given for the healing of spirit, mind, and body" (Book of Common Prayer, page 861).

Outward and Visible Sign

The outward and visible sign of healing is anointing with oil and/or the laying on of hands. Oil has been used for therapeutic purposes since antiquity. The Good Samaritan bandaged with oil and wine the wounds of the one who had been robbed. The disciples anointed the sick with oil. Oil seeps into the pores of the skin, penetrating deep into the body. Jesus' healings highlight the healing power of touch. Jesus rubbed spit into the eyes of a blind man and brought his sight back. A sick woman touched Jesus' robe and was healed.

Jesus put his fingers into the ears of a deaf man and restored his hearing. Indeed, the caring touch of another can provide both comfort and healing.

Inward and Spiritual Grace

Healing is a sacrament of faith that follows the healing in the ministry of Jesus. Through healing, Jesus made life whole and proclaimed the restoration of God's kingdom. Healing raises up the sick to God's healing power, which brings the strength, courage, and peace needed to face the realities of our broken world, including disease and mental and physical pain. Sickness weakens the spirit. Healing seeks to strengthen the spirit. Sickness isolates individuals. Healing seeks to restore the sick to community, bringing a wholeness of all members. Sickness brings despair. Healing seeks to renew hope.

> The outward sign of healing is laying on of hands and anointing with oil. The inward grace is healing of body, mind, and spirit.

Healing can be done privately or publicly. Many churches offer healing as part of, or shortly after, the Sunday service. During the Rite of Healing, the priest lays his or her hands upon the person and prays to God for healing. If anointing is offered, the priest dips a thumb in the oil and makes the sign of the cross on the person's forehead and anoints in the name of the Father and of the Son and of the Holy Spirit.

It is important to remember that healing is for brokenness brought about by disease and sin. We are called to repent of our sins and seek restored relationships. Healing through laying on of hands helps to restore inner brokenness and soothe a suffering spirit. Through the laying on of hands and anointing with oil, Christ and Christ's healing power is made present to us.

ORDINATION

Then Jesus went about all the cities and villages, teaching in their synagogues, and proclaiming the good news of the kingdom, and curing every disease and every sickness. When he saw the crowds, he had compassion for them, because they were harassed and helpless, like sheep without a shepherd. Then he said to his disciples, "The harvest is plentiful, but the laborers are few; therefore ask the Lord of the harvest to send out laborers into his harvest."

(Matthew 9:35–38)

This passage from the Gospel according to Matthew, through the ministry of Jesus, provides a vision of church leadership dedicated to teaching, proclaiming the good news, and caring for the people. Faced with the crowds, "like sheep without a shepherd" Jesus recognizes the need for servant-laborers to serve the people. **Ordination** is a gift from God for the care and nurture of his people and for the proclamation of the Gospel.

Three Holy Orders

All baptized Christians are called to represent Christ and work toward reconciliation in the world. Some are also called to holy orders of bishop, priest, or deacon. We understand this call as originating from God and acknowledged and validated by the individual and his or her community of believers.

Ordained ministers serve as living reminders of the church's life and mission. Bishops are a symbol of unity, catholicity, and apostolicity of the church. Priests are a sign of the priesthood of the entire church. Deacons are a sign of the church as servants to the world. Bishops, priests, and deacons serve the church so that we, the laity, can serve as the body of Christ to the world.

The primary ministry of the **bishop** (and all ministers) is to "represent Christ and his church." The unique ministry of the bishop is to oversee a diocese as apostle, chief priest, and pastor. As a successor to the apostles, a bishop symbolizes the unity of the priesthood throughout time and, with other bishops, symbolizes the unity of the church. Bishops guard and teach the faith and are charged with proclaiming the word of God. Bishops alone have the authority to ordain priests and deacons, to confirm the baptized, and to bless a church.

Bishops and priests represent Christ as a shepherd who cares for his sheep.

A **priest** serves the church primarily as pastor to the people. A priest shares the responsibility of overseeing the church with the bishop. In that role, priests celebrate Holy Eucharist and baptize. A priest also blesses and grants absolution of sins in the name of God. Priests are given the role of teaching and proclaiming the Gospel, a ministry they share with the laity.

A **deacon** assists the bishop and priests in their liturgical, pastoral, and teaching roles. During Holy Eucharist, deacons read the Gospel, lead the intercessions, and assist in the preparation of the table. Deacons have the special responsibility of serving the poor, the sick, the suffering, and the helpless.

The Sacrament of Ordination

A person who is called by God and recognized by the church to the ordained ministry is ordained by prayer and the laying on of hands by a bishop. A bishop is consecrated by the laying on of hands by three bishops.

The laying on of hands is the outward and visible sign of ordination. The inward and spiritual grace is the authority granted by power of the Holy Spirit to minister to the church.

The Rite of Ordination reflects the preparation a candidate must undertake. Let's explore the Rite of Ordination of a priest. First, a priest and a layperson present the candidate to the bishop. Candidates are presented because the call by God to ordination is a call that is identified by both the individual and the community. The process of preparing for ordination takes at least eighteen months and includes identifying the call but also theological training, practical experience, emotional development, and spiritual formation. At ordination, the presenters state their belief that the candidate is qualified and suitable for the ordained ministry.

After the presentation, the candidate declares belief that the holy scriptures are the word of God and contain all things necessary to salvation and promises to conform to the doctrine, discipline, and worship of the church. Finally, the people express their desire that the candidate be ordained and promise to uphold him or her in the ministry. Like all the sacraments, ordination is celebrated in community. This recognizes that we are one body in Christ.

Before consecration, the candidate is examined by the bishop to determine a true calling and promises to pursue the disciplines necessary to fulfill the ministry. The bishop ends the examination by asking God to grant the candidate the grace and power to fulfill those promises.

At the consecration the bishop says the prayer of consecration in which the bishop gives praise and thanksgiving to God for his love, his call to us, and his gift of Jesus, the risen Christ. Together with the priests present, the bishop lays hands on the candidate and asks God to grant the candidate the power and grace of the Holy Spirit to make him or her a priest in the church. The power and grace of the Holy Spirit is the inward and spiritual grace of the sacrament of ordination.

Once and Always a Deacon, Priest, or Bishop

Ordination confers a lifelong ministry. Barring renunciation of priestly vows or deposition of an ordained person from ordained ministry, regardless of whether the ordained has a paid position in the church, the ordained will continue as ordained persons until death.

ADDITIONAL PASTORAL OFFICES

The Book of Common Prayer provides pastoral rites for other key times of life. Two are Ministration at the Time of Death (page 462) and Burial of the Dead (page 469). A third is Thanksgiving for a Child (page 439).

Ministration of the Sick and the Burial of the Dead

We pray for God to deliver the dying from evil, sin, and all tribulation. We ask that the dying rest with the saints and with the Father, Son, and Holy Spirit. Burial is not a sacrament because the person is no longer physically present and therefore is not in need of a physical sign of God's grace. In the midst of sorrow, the Burial of the Dead reminds us of the joy of the Easter promise. We celebrate life that depends on God and pray for eternal life in Christ.

Thanksgiving for the Birth or Adoption of a Child

With this rite, a congregation welcomes a new member of a family and gives thanks to God for creation. In it we recognize the bonds of family, and the priest blesses the child and the community for their life together. This service is independent of baptism.

CONCLUSION

As physical and spiritual beings we live sacramental lives. God's grace is given to us every day through signs of God's dwelling with us. God uses material things to reach out to us in many ways; the embrace of a friend, a gentle smile, table fellowship, and the blessing of a mother to her child are just a few examples. Open your eyes to the world and God's actions in it. Look for the rainbows. Visible signs will sustain your hope and provide you the grace to live in the newness and fullness of life. Opening your eyes to God's abundant graces will bring you ever closer to union with God.

✠ TRANSFORMING QUESTIONS

1. **Be Attentive:** Think of a time when you participated in a sacrament. What happened? Who was present? What were you thinking and feeling? Be as detailed in your description as you are able.

2. **Be Intelligent:** What did that sacrament mean to you? Did you notice an inward change?

3. **Be Reasonable:** Share your experience with a friend, and invite your friend to share an experience with you. What did that experience mean for your friend? Does your friend's experience suggest a new way for you to understand the sacrament?

4. **Be Responsible:** As a result of this reflection, what might you do differently? What might you continue doing? What support do you need for this?

5. **Be in Love Transformed:** Bring your reflection to the next sacrament you experience.

Glossary

Numbers included with each entry
refer to pages on which the term is discussed.

Acts of the General Convention. Legislation passed by General Convention that governs the common life of all Episcopal churches. (100)

Adoration. Words and actions that express our love for God and creation. (128)

Advent. The first season of the church year, during which we prepare for Christ's coming into the world and Christ's return. (164)

Alb. A white garment worn by bishops, priests, deacons, and acolytes during the entire liturgy. (163)

Altar. The table within the sanctuary around which Holy Communion is celebrated. (161)

Anamnesis. An active form of memory that connects the past to the present in a way that allows us to become a present participant in a past event. (175)

Anglican Communion. Forty-four independently governed churches in more than 160 countries that share a common faith, history, and tradition. (101)

Anglican Consultative Council. A gathering of laypeople, bishops, priests, and deacons from provinces in the Anglican Communion. The Anglican Consultative Council is the only incorporated body of the Anglican Communion. (102

Anglican prayer beads. A set of thirty-three beads joined together into a circular pattern used along with words of prayer. (134)

Antiphon. A sentence, usually from the Bible, said before and after the psalm. (130)

Apocrypha. Books and writings added to the Bible in the sixteenth century by the Roman Catholic Church. Not all Christians recognize the Apocrypha as holy scripture. (44)

Apostles' Creed. The earliest formal statement of Christian belief. The Apostles' Creed is said during baptism, Morning Prayer, and Evening Prayer. (72)

Apostolic. An adjective that describes something as continuing in the teaching and fellowship of the apostles. The church is apostolic. (87)

Apostolic succession. The passing of authority by apostles to local leaders with the laying on of hands. Episcopal bishops today are the successors in an unbroken line of ministry to the apostles. (55)

Archbishop of Canterbury. The primate of the Church of England. The archbishop of Canterbury is first among equals and has the right of invitation and recognition of other Anglican provinces to the Anglican Communion. (102)

Ayres, Anne. 1816–1896. First American religious sister in the Anglican tradition. With a few other sisters organized the Sisterhood of the Holy Communion in 1852. (66)

Baptism. Full initiation by water and the Holy Spirit into the body of Christ and the church. (172)

Baptismal covenant. A statement that affirms belief in the triune God followed by five promises to follow in the Christian fellowship, resist evil, proclaim the good news, serve Christ in all persons, and strive for justice and peace. The congregation renews the Baptismal Covenant with candidates for baptism. (17)

Baptismal font. The container inside or at the entrance of a church that holds the waters of baptism. (161)

Baptismal promises. Five promises candidates for baptism make about how they will live their lives as members of the body of Christ. See the answers to questions 4–8 of the Baptismal Covenant on pages 304 and 305 of the Book of Common Prayer. (22, 107)

Bible. A collection of sixty-six books of the Jewish scriptures (Old Testament) and the Christian scriptures (New Testament) that reveal God's creative and redeeming actions throughout history. Also called holy scriptures. (29)

Bishop. One of three ordained orders of ministry in the church. A bishop serves the offices of apostle, chief priest, and pastor of a diocese. A bishop suffragan, a bishop coadjutor, or bishop assisting assists bishops diocesan in large dioceses. (185)

Book of Common Prayer. Provides the liturgies, prayers, and instructions so that all members of the church may share in common worship. First established in England in 1549 by the Act of Uniformity. The American Book of Common Prayer was first adopted in 1789 by the First General Convention of the Episcopal Church. (60)

Brent, Charles Henry. 1862–1929. A priest who led the Episcopal Church in the ecumenical movement that established the first meeting of the World Council of Churches in 1948. (64)

Burgess, John. 1909–2003. The first African American to serve as bishop of a diocese in the Episcopal Church. (65)

Calvin, John. 1509–64. A French leader of the Reformation. Calvin wrote a systematic theology that rejected the authority of the pope, accepted justification by grace through faith, and expressed a fundamental doctrine of predestination. The doctrine of predestination is the belief that God directs the course of history to the minutest detail. According to this doctrine, humankind's role in creation is to maintain the order created by God. (56)

Canon. (1) The collection of books recognized as holy scripture. (2) The written rules of the Episcopal Church for its governance. (3) Title of assistant priests at a cathedral. (34, 94)

Canons of the Episcopal Church. The written rules that govern the Episcopal Church. (91)

Canticle. A "little song" based on scripture used in worship. See pages 144–45 of the Book of Common Prayer for a list of suggested canticles for Morning and Evening Prayer. (130)

Catechumen. Someone who is in the process of preparing for baptism. The process includes learning Christian beliefs and practices and discerning a desire to become a member of the church. (173)

Cathedral. The designation of the church that houses the cathedra, the bishop's seat. The cathedral is the principal church of the diocese. (93)

Catholic. A term that means universal. We say that the church is catholic because it is a faith for all people and for all time. (79, 87)

Centering prayer. A prayer of quieting and stillness to know the presence of God. Developed by the Desert Fathers and Mothers and revived by Trappist monk Thomas Keating. (131)

Chalice. A cup for the wine at Eucharist. (155)

Chancel. The area of the church that contains the pulpit, lectern, and altar, and is often raised in elevation and separated from the nave by a rail or screen. Often called the sanctuary. (160)

Chasuble. A long poncho-like garment worn by the celebrant over the alb during the Eucharist. (163)

Christian scriptures. A collection of twenty-seven books written by early Christians that proclaim the good news of Jesus Christ and tell of the early history of the church. (31)

Christmas. The season of the church year during which we celebrate the birth of Christ. It begins on Christmas Day and ends twelve days later on January 6, Epiphany. (164)

Coeternal. Two or more things that can be understood only in relationship to one another as part of a whole. They exist together at all times into eternity. (74)

Collect. A short prayer that "collects" the themes of the day. Collects vary according to the day, the season of the church year, and the occasion, and can be found in services in the Book of Common Prayer. (152)

Communicant. Member of a church who has received communion at least three times in a year. (91)

Communicant in good standing. A communicant who has been "faithful in working, praying, and giving for the spread of the kingdom of God." (91)

Confession. Prayer in which we admit that we have done something wrong, turn away from sin, and seek to restore our relationship with others through God. (128)

Confirmation. The rite in which a baptized person makes a mature commitment to Christ and receives continuing strength from the Holy Spirit. (177)

Corporal. A white square of cloth on which the bread and wine are placed during the Eucharistic Prayer. (155)

Covenant. An agreement entered into freely by two or more parties. A covenant with God is a relationship initiated by God and responded to by people in faith. (18)

Cranmer, Thomas. 1489–1556. Archbishop of Canterbury during the reigns of Henry VIII and Edward VI. Compiled the first Book of Common Prayer. (57)

Crosier (also spelled crozier). A staff that symbolizes the pastoral ministry of the bishop. (163)

Daily Office. A set of prayers and readings that mark the times of the day. (128)

Daniels, Jonathan. 1939–1965. A young European American Episcopal seminarian martyred in the civil rights movement. (65)

Deacon. One of three ordained orders of ministry in the church. A deacon is called to be a servant to those in need and to assist the bishop and priests in proclaiming the Gospel and administering the sacraments. (185)

Dean. The lead clergyperson at a cathedral. (94)

Diocesan Convention. Annual meeting of all parishes within a diocese. Similar to an annual meeting for a parish, but for the diocese. (94)

Diocesan Council. A group of priests and laypersons elected from within a diocese along with the bishop to act on behalf of Diocesan Convention during the year. (94)

Diocese. Basic administrative unit of the Episcopal Church. Individual churches act in accordance with the rules of, and share a common mission with, their diocese. The jurisdiction of a bishop diocesan. (92)

Discernment. A process of understanding. As a Christian practice, discernment is a process of prayerful reflection in which we come to understand our spiritual gifts and God's call to ministry. ()119)

Easter. A season of the church year during which we celebrate the resurrection of Christ. Begins with Easter Sunday and lasts fifty days. (166)

Enmegahbowh. 1807–1902. First Native American priest ordained in the Episcopal Church. Worked among the Ojibway peoples in Minnesota. (61)

Epiclesis. Words that ask God to send the Holy Spirit to make the bread and the wine holy so that they will be the body and blood of Christ. (60, 157)

Epiphany. The day on which we celebrate the visit of the Magi to the Christ Child. Also a season of the church year in which we celebrate the divinity of Jesus beginning with Jesus' baptism and ending with the Transfiguration. (165)

Epistles. A set of twenty-one writings, many which are in the form of letters addressed to early Christian communities or individuals. The Epistles are part of the Christian scriptures. (36)

Executive Council. An elected body of people charged with "the coordination, development, and implementation of the ministry and mission of the Church." It acts on behalf of General Convention. (98)

Fasting. Actively choosing not to do something for a short period of time so that we may draw our attention to God. (143)

Fraction anthem. A hymn sung at the breaking of the bread. (157)

General Convention. The highest legislative body of the Episcopal Church, which meets once every three years to approve the Episcopal Church's programs and budget. (95)

Gifts of the Spirit. Talents and abilities God gives us to fulfill our ministry. (115)

Gloria. A song of praise to God in the service of Holy Eucharist. (152)

Gospels. Four books in the Christian scriptures (Matthew, Mark, Luke, and John), which proclaim the good news of salvation through Jesus Christ by telling about Jesus' ministry, teaching, death, and resurrection. (41)

Great Commandments. You shall love the Lord your God with all your heart, with all your soul, and with all your mind, and you shall love your neighbor as yourself. (82)

Great Commission. The charge by Jesus in the Gospel according to Matthew to the disciples to "go and make disciples of all nations." (53)

Great Thanksgiving. The name given for the Eucharistic Prayer. Also known as the prayer of consecration. (156)

Harris, Barbara Clementine. 1930–. First woman consecrated bishop in the Episcopal Church. Consecrated bishop suffragan of the Diocese of Massachusetts in 1989. Known also for her commitment to civil rights issues and justice. (67)

Healing of the Sick. The rite of anointing the sick with oil, or the laying on of hands, by which God's grace is given for the healing of spirit, mind, and body. Also called unction of the sick. (183)

Henry VIII. 1491–1547. King of England who issued the Act of Supremacy, which made the king the head of the Church of England and severed the ties between the Church of England and the Roman Catholic Church. (57)

Hobart, John Henry. 1775–1830. Led early efforts to grow the Episcopal Church. During his time as bishop of New York, the number of churches in his diocese more than tripled and the number of clergy quintupled. (60)

Holy Eucharist. The principal act of Christian worship, in which we remember the life, death, and resurrection of Jesus Christ and proclaim that we await his coming in glory. (151)

Holy Matrimony. The physical and spiritual binding together of two people before God and his people for mutual joy and with the intention of a lifelong commitment. (178)

Holy Spirit. God's power and presence in our history, in our present, and in our future. The Holy Spirit is the third person of the Trinity. (79)

House of Bishops. The gathering of all bishops at General Convention to consider legislation and between conventions for worship, prayer, study, and dialogue. The House of Bishops meets twice each year between General Convention and often issues pastoral statements that provide guidance and advice to the church. (98)

House of Deputies. One of two legislative bodies of the Episcopal Church. (The House of Bishops is the other legislative body.) The House of Deputies comprises a group of clergy and laypeople elected by the Diocesan Convention in every diocese. (98)

Icons. Visual images that point beyond themselves. Icons are commonly used in the practice of prayer. (138)

Ignatian Examen. A specific process of discernment developed by Ignatius of Loyola in the sixteenth century based on the belief that we can understand God's desires for us in the context of our daily lives. (122)

Incarnation. The belief that Jesus was God in the flesh. (77)

Intercessions. Prayers in which we request God's blessings and grace for others. (128)

Invitatory. A sentence and response that opens our hearts and minds to the purpose of the gathering. (129)

Jesus Prayer. A mantra, "Lord, Jesus Christ, son of God, have mercy on me, a sinner." (133)

Jewish scriptures. A collection of thirty-nine books that form the first part of the Bible and tell the stories of the Hebrew people and their covenant relationship with God. Also called the Old Testament. (31)

Jones, Absalom. 1746–1818. First African American priest ordained in the Episcopal Church. Born a slave, he bought his own freedom and the freedom of his wife. With Richard Allen, Jones established the Free African Society, the first organized African American society in the United States. (61)

Justification by grace through faith. A doctrine set forth by Martin Luther that salvation is a gift from God. Individuals need only respond in faith to accept salvation. (56)

Kemper, Jackson. 1789–1870. First missionary bishop in 1835 serving in the western territories of the United States during the mid-1800s. He encouraged the translation of services into native languages and pleaded for more attention to Native Americans. His unofficial title is "The Bishop of the Whole Northwest." (61)

Labyrinth. A sacred pattern in the shape of a circle with one path that winds to the center and back out again. A famous labyrinth is the eleven circuit labyrinth on the floor of Chartres Cathedral in France. (142)

Lambeth Conference. A gathering of Anglican bishops held every ten years at Lambeth Palace, the official residence of the archbishop of Canterbury. (102)

Laypersons. The people of God called to carry on Christ's work of reconciliation in the world according to the gifts given to them. Most of the ministry of the laity occurs outside the church. Laypersons may also perform ministries within the church. (88)

Lectio divina. A four-step process of prayerfully reading the word of God. *Lectio divina* is a method of reading for prayerful devotion rather than scholarly study. (138)

Lectionary. A three-year cycle of scripture readings for use in public worship. The Book of Common Prayer includes two lectionaries — a lectionary for Sundays and the Daily Office lectionary. Many Episcopal churches follow the Revised Common Lectionary for Sunday readings. (46, 153)

Lent. The season of the church year during which we prepare for the resurrection of Jesus. It is a time of prayer, fasting, and penitence. It begins on Ash Wednesday and ends on Holy Saturday, the day before Easter. (165)

Liturgy. The rites (prayers) and actions that define our common worship as a community. (150)

Luther, Martin. 1483–1546. A German leader of the Reformation. He posted ninety-five theses on the door of the castle church in Wittenberg, inviting others to oppose practices by the Roman Catholic Church. One abusive practice he opposed was the church's selling indulgences to sinners as proof of their repentance necessary for salvation. One of Luther's more famous doctrines is the doctrine of justification by grace through faith. This doctrine stated that sacraments, good works, and the mediation of the church were not necessary for salvation and put individuals in direct connection with God. (56)

Mandala. A circular pattern of lines and colors used as a tool for prayer. (140)

Mantras. Sacred words or phrases said repeatedly for a period of time. (133)

Memorial. An act or object that preserves the memory of a person or event. In the context of Eucharist, memorial is declaring that Christ is among us, a living sacrifice, for us today. (175)

Memorial Acclamation. Words of praise by the people (Christ has died. Christ is risen. Christ will come again.) said after the words of institution during the Great Thanksgiving. (156)

Middle Ages. A period of time from the fall of the Roman Empire in the fifth century to the rise of the Renaissance in the fifteenth century. During the Middle Ages there was a strict division of social classes, and land was largely controlled by nobles and the church. Without a strong and stable political force, Christianity became the leading force in Western civilization. (55)

Ministry. The Christian calling to serve. (109)

Miter. A tall, pointed hat worn by the bishop. (Also spelled mitre.) (163)

Monastic community. A group of people who believe in God and live in community with others separate from society. They dedicate themselves to simple lives of service and prayer ordered by a common rule of life. (129)

Muhlenberg, William Augustus. 1796–1877. Leading priest in the Episcopal Church in the nineteenth century, who was concerned that the church minister to all social groups. (62)

Nave. The large vertical area of a cross-shaped church where worshipers gather. The nave lies between the chancel and the narthex. (161)

New covenant. The relationship established with God through Jesus Christ in which God promises to bring us into the kingdom of God. We promise to believe in Christ and keep his commandments to love God and our neighbors as ourselves. (20, 82)

New Testament. See Christian scriptures.

Oakerhater, David Pendleton. 1850–1931. First Cheyenne deacon in the Episcopal Church. He founded schools and missions throughout Oklahoma. (61)

Old Covenant. The relationship God established with the Hebrews in which he would be their God and they would be his people. They promised to love justice, do mercy, and walk humbly with their God. (81)

Old Testament. See Jewish scriptures.

Opening acclamation. The greeting to God's family that begins the service of Holy Eucharist and proclaims in whose name we gather. (152)

Ordination. The sacrament by which God gives authority and the grace of the Holy Spirit through prayer and the laying on of hands to those being made bishops, priests, and deacons. (185)

Oxford Movement. A movement in the nineteenth century to revive earlier Roman Catholic liturgical practices. (63)

Parables. Stories used as metaphors for teaching. The synoptic Gospels present Jesus as teaching with parables. (42)

Parish. A group of people who have incorporated as a congregation within the church and who worship regularly, participate in the sacraments, and support one another in their Christian lives. (91)

Paschal Triduum. The three days of Easter. Begins with the Maundy Thursday service in the evening, continues with Good Friday, and peaks with the Great Easter Vigil, the first service of Easter day. (165)

Paten. A small plate for the bread at Eucharist. (155)

Pentateuch. The first five books of the Bible: Genesis, Exodus, Leviticus, Numbers, and Deuteronomy. The word is derived from two Greek words — *pen* meaning "five" and *tecuho* meaning "book." (35)

Pentecost. The fiftieth day after Easter on which we celebrate the birth of the church. Also, the season after Pentecost Sunday and before Advent. (53)

Petition. Prayer in which we request God's blessings and grace for ourselves. (128)

Prayer. The experience of the presence of God through words, actions, or silence. Forms of prayer are adoration, confession, thanksgiving, intercession, and petition. (127)

Presiding bishop. The national church's chief pastor and representative to the world. (98)

Priest. One of three ordained orders of ministry in the church. Priests administer the sacraments, proclaim the Gospel, serve as pastor to the people, and, with the bishop, oversee the church. (185)

Primate. The chief bishop of a national Anglican Church. The primate of the Episcopal Church is also called the presiding bishop. (101)

Primates' Meeting. An annual gathering of the primates of all provinces in the Anglican Communion. (102)

Psalms. A book of hymns in the Bible. Psalms is the only book of the Bible included in its entirety in the Book of Common Prayer. (40)

Rainsford, William. 1850–1933. Episcopal priest active in social ministry in the late nineteenth and early twentieth centuries. (62)

Real Presence. The belief that Christ's body and blood are present in the consecrated bread and wine. By eating the communion bread and drinking the wine we are made one with Christ. (174)

Reconciliation of a Penitent (also simply reconciliation). The sacrament of confessing one's sins to a priest and receiving assurance of pardon and the grace of absolution. (180)

Rector. A priest who leads a parish church. (91)

Reformation. A religious movement of the sixteenth century that began as an attempt to reform the Roman Catholic Church and resulted in the establishment of Protestant churches. The Reformation addressed what were perceived to be abuses of power by the Roman Catholic Church that had developed during the Middle Ages. (56)

Ritual memory. The recollection of actions that deepen our experiences as they are repeated. (140)

Robinson, V. Gene. 1947–. First openly gay priest to be consecrated a bishop in the Episcopal Church. Consecrated the ninth bishop of the Diocese of New Hampshire in 2004. (68)

Rubrics. Directions for liturgies printed in italics in the Book of Common Prayer. (151)

Rule of life. A set of guidelines for living that aid in keeping our lives in balance with God as the center. (145)

Sacrament. An outward and visible sign of inward and spiritual grace, given by Christ as sure and certain means by which we receive that grace. (See the Book of Common Prayer, page 857.) (170)

Sanctus. A hymn of praise beginning with the words "Holy, Holy, Holy" and sung during the Great Thanksgiving. (156)

Schori, Katherine Jefferts. First woman elected presiding bishop of the Episcopal Church (2006). (67)

Seabury, Samuel. 1729–96. The first American bishop of the Anglican Church. Consecrated by Scottish bishops in November 1784. (59)

Season after Pentecost. The weeks during the church year after Pentecost Sunday and before the first Sunday of Advent. The Season after Pentecost is a time for growing in faith. (166)

Shema. The Hebrew declaration of faith in one God: Hear, O Israel: The LORD is our God, the LORD alone (Deuteronomy 6:4). (37)

Sin. Falling short of God's will. (83)

Spiritual direction. The art of helping others explore a deeper relationship with God. (145)

Spiritual disciplines. Intentional practices that keep us in dialogue with God. (127)

Stole. A narrow width of cloth worn by bishops and priests over both shoulders and by a deacon over the left shoulder. (164)

Sursum corda. A Eucharistic dialogue between the celebrant and the people in which the people lift their hearts to the Lord. The *Sursum corda* begins the Great Thanksgiving. (156)

Thanksgiving. Prayer in which we express our gratitude to God for all the blessings and mercies God gives us. (128)

Transept. The horizontal parts of a cross-shaped church extending out from the nave and the chancel. (161)

Transubstantiation. The belief that when consecrated, the substance of the bread and the wine are transformed into the substance of Christ's body and blood, while the appearance as bread and wine continues to be unchanged. (175)

Trinity. The belief in one God who exists in three eternal, distinct, and equal persons. (74)

Trisagion. The prayer, "Holy God, Holy and Mighty, Holy Immortal One, have mercy on me." (133)

Tyndale, William. 1494–1536. First person to translate the Bible from the original Hebrew and Greek into English. (57)

Vestments. Special clothing worn by leaders of worship. The celebrant, for example, wears a chasuble during Holy Eucharist. (163)

Vestry. Leaders of a parish elected to supervise and make decisions, particularly about the finances and buildings and grounds, between annual meetings. The vestry also provides the planning and organization needed to support the mission of a local parish. (91)

Words of institution. The words that tell the story of the Last Supper. (156)

World Council of Churches. A fellowship of more than 340 churches worldwide that works toward the unity of the church. (64)

Worship. A response of praise and thanksgiving to the God who creates us, blesses us, and loves us. (149)

References

The *Anglican Communion*. Pamphlet. Communications Department of the Anglican Communion, 2004.

Artress, Lauren. *Walking a Sacred Path.* New York: Riverhead Books, 1995.

Augustine of Hippo. *The Confessions.* Book 1, chapter 1. Trans. J. G. Pilkington, in *and Post-Nicene Fathers,* ed. Philip Schaff. Grand Rapids, Mich.: Eerdmans Publishing, 1886.

Bauman, Lynn C. *The Anglican Rosary.* Telephone, Tex.: Praxis, 2003.

Berlin, Adele, and Marc Avi Brettler, eds. *The Jewish Study Bible.* Oxford: Oxford University Press, 2004.

The Book of Common Prayer. New York: Church Publishing, 1979.

Borg, Marcus. *The Heart of Christianity.* New York: HarperCollins, 2003.

The Budget for the Episcopal Church, 2007–2009. General Convention.

Constitutions and Canons Together with the Rules of Order for the Government of the Protestant Episcopal Church in the United States of America Otherwise Known as The Episcopal Church. New York: Church Publishing, 2006.

Dillard, Annie. *Teaching a Stone to Talk.* New York: Harper & Row Publishers, 1982.

Dozier, Verna. *The Dream of God.* Boston: Cowley Publications, 1991.

Edwards, Lloyd. *Discerning Your Spiritual Gifts.* Cambridge, Mass.: Cowley Publications, 1988.

The Episcopal Church Annual. Pittsburgh, Pa.: Morehouse Publishing, 2008.

Episcopal Fast Facts. Pamphlet. Office of Communications of the Episcopal Church, 2007.

Farrington, Debra K. "Balancing Life by the Rule." *Spirituality & Health* (Winter 2001): 44.

———. *Hearing with the Heart: A Gentle Guide to Discerning God's Will for Your Life.* San Francisco: Jossey-Bass, 2003.

Ferlo, Roger. *Opening the Bible.* Boston: Cowley Publications, 1997.

Foster, Richard J. *Celebration of Discipline.* New York: HarperCollins, 1988.

Frankl, Victor. "The Search for Meaning." *Saturday Review* (September 13, 1958).

Gomes, Peter J. *The Good Book: Reading the Bible with Mind and Heart.* San Francisco: HarperSanFrancisco, 1996.

Green Graham. *Brighton Rock.* New York: Viking Press, 1938.

Guenther, Margaret. *The Practice of Prayer.* The New Church Teaching Series, vol. 4. Cambridge, Mass.: Cowley Publications, 1998.

Hatchett, Marion J. *Commentary on the American Prayer Book.* San Francisco: HarperCollins Publisher, 1995.

Hughes, Robert. *A Jerk on One End: Reflections of a Mediocre Fisherman.* London: Harvill Press, 1999.

Kater, John L. "The Persistence of the Gospel." Unpublished manuscript.

Keating, Thomas. *Open Mind, Open Heart.* New York: Continuum, 2000.

Kitch, Anne E. *The Anglican Family Prayer Book*. Harrisburg, Pa.: Morehouse Publishing, 2004.

Klein, Patricia S. *Worship without Words*. Brewster, Mass.: Paraclete Press, 2000.

Kuyawa-Holbrook, Sheryl, ed. *Freedom Is a Dream: A Documentary History of Women in the Episcopal Church*. New York: Church Publishing, 2002.

Lee, Jeffrey. *Opening the Prayer Book*. Boston: Cowley Publications, 1999.

Lesser Feasts and Fasts 2005. New York: Church Publishing, 2008.

Linn, Dennis, Sheila Fabricant Linn, and Matthew Linn. *Sleeping with Bread: Holding What Gives You Life*. Mahwah, N.J.: Paulist Press, 1995.

Lonergan, Bernard. "Dialectic of Authority." In *Third Collection*. New York: Paulist Press, 1985.

Malloy, Patrick. *Celebrating the Eucharist*. New York: Church Publishing, 2008.

Marshall, Paul V. "Has Your Religion Helped You Grow Up?" *Allentown (Pa.) Morning Call*, July 31, 2004, D9.

———. "When an Ending Is a Beginning." *Diocesan Life*, Bethlehem, Pa. (May 1997).

Mays, James L., ed. *Bible Commentary*. San Francisco: HarperSanFrancisco, 2000.

Nouwen, Henri. *Clowning in Rome*. New York: Doubleday, 1979.

Platter, Ormonde. *Many Servants*. Boston: Cowley Publications, 2004.

Post, Ellwood, W. *Saints, Signs, and Symbols*. Harrisburg, Pa.: Morehouse Publishing, 1962, 1974.

Prothero, Stephen. *Religious Literacy: What Every American Needs to Know — and Doesn't*. New York: HarperCollins, 2007.

Roberts, Tom. "Mysterious Freedoms and a Wild Holy." *Bethlehem (Pa.) Globe-Times*, 1978.

Smith, Martin L. *Reconciliation: Preparing for Confession in the Episcopal Church*. Boston: Cowley Publications, 1985.

Stravinskas, Peter M. J. *Understanding the Sacraments: A Guide for Prayer and Study*. San Francisco: Ignatius Press, 1997.

Thompsett, Fredrica Harris. *Living with History*. Boston: Cowley Publications, 1999.

Sources Cited in Chapter Introductions

Frankl, Viktor E. *Man's Search for Meaning*. New York: Pocket Publisher, rev. updated ed., 1997.

Liddy, Richard. *Startling Strangeness: Reading Lonergan's Insight*. Lanham, Md.: University Press of America, 2006.

Lonergan, Bernard. *Insight: A Study of Human Understanding (Collected Works of Bernard Lonergan)*. Toronto: University of Toronto Press, 5th ed., 1992

———. *Method in Theology*. Toronto: University of Toronto Press, 2d ed., 1990.

The Lonergan Website: A Virtual Place for Collaboration in Lonergan Studies. http://lonergan .concordia.ca/.

Tekippe, Terry. *What Is Lonergan Up to in Insight?* Collegeville, Minn.: Liturgical Press, 1996.

———. *Bernard Lonergan: An Introductory Guide to Insight*. Mahwah, N.J.: Paulist Press, 2003.

Tillich, Paul. *The Courage to Be*. New Haven, Conn.: Yale University Press, 2nd rev. ed., 2000.

Acknowledgments

Queen Elizabeth: page 58, John J. Anderson, *A School History of England* (New York: Effingham Maynard & Co., 1889). Edited by Florida Center for Instructional Technology. Used with permission.

Absalom Jones: page 61, by Raphaelle Peale, 1810, oil on paper mounted to board, Delaware Art Museum. Gift of Absalom Jones School, 1971. Reproduced with permission.

Most Rev. Katharine Jefferts Schori: page 67, Getty Images. Used by permission.

Map of Provinces of the Episcopal Church: page 96, courtesy of the Domestic and Foreign Missionary Society of the Protestant Episcopal Church. Used with permission.

Anglican prayer beads: page 135, by Frank Logue. Used with permission.

Rublev's fourteenth-century Russian icon: page 138. Tretiakov Gallery, Moscow. Public domain.

The labyrinth: page 142, from Veriditas (*veriditas.net*). Used with permission.

Symbol of reconciliation: page 180, created by Episcopal artist Jan Neal. Used with permission.

Artwork on pages 152, 155, 156, 160, 161, 164, 165 by Dorothy Thomson Perez in Patrick Malloy, *Celebrating the Eucharist* (New York: Church Publishing, 2007). Used with permission.

Artwork on pages 16, 24, 42, 74, 77, 117, 140, 173, 174, 177, 179, 185 by C. E. Visminas Co., Ltd. Morehouse Publishing. Used with permission.